The

President's Book

Experiencing the Essentials with Six Board Presidents

Donna Alvarado

Alan Radnor

Kathy Ransier

Teckie Shackelford

Warren Tyler

Carole Williams

with Donn F. Vickers

Carole Williams, Editor

Elizabeth Jewell, Editorial Assistant

ACKNOWLEDGEMENTS

Behind each of us is a trail of boards (mostly happy) where we have worked, wrestled, and wondered about matters of great and small importance. That has been our fertile ground of training. Whatever we may now know or be able to do or value is because of those fine and forbearing executives and board members who have been our colleagues in one good cause or another. And through the fortuitous merger of our six diverse trails, we have found commonality of experience and insights we hope will be of value to others embarking on similar presidential journeys.

Perhaps with less than appropriate humility we salute one another. Over the months of retreating, writing, advancing, and rewriting, we have come to cherish the rich and varied presidential voices and insights that reside among us.

Acknowledgement passes into appreciation when we think of Donn Vickers who most of the time got down in writing the best of what we said. That appreciation is warmly extended to Carole Williams and Elizabeth Jewell who all of the time got it organized, transcribed, and edited with remarkable promptness and propriety.

Our additional thanks to Don and Teckie Shackelford for believing this project would be worthwhile and acting on that belief with their generous financial support.

Our conviction is that what you have agreed to do is most significant and that you deserve assistance and satisfaction in the doing of it. Our hope is that you will find something on the pages that follow that will inform, enhance, and enliven your term as board president.

January 2001
Columbus, Ohio

TABLE OF CONTENTS

Part 1

First Things First

Chapter 1

Starting Somewhere

Y ou do have to start somewhere and we'd like to start by raising your sights above the dreary details of bylaws and the confounding tangle of perceived policies. We'd like to start with the remarkable opportunity you have to shape the life of your organization. We'd like to suggest that you choose to lead and that your leadership be focused on the large opportunities and enthusiasms. Of course, you will do this in partnership with your executive. And of course, you will seek and incorporate the insights of your board, but there is yet more. As board president you have been entrusted with the responsibility of embracing and embodying the initial flame that founded your organization. So your job is more about the dynamic than the detail, more about the big picture than the small, more about vision than management.

And we say this with confidence not really knowing you. Maybe you are starting your second year as president and, because of the way much of the first year went, have mixed feelings about the twelve months ahead. At times, you've felt like the executive really runs the place and there's little need for someone called president. Then other times big decisions were unexpectedly dumped in your lap and you weren't sure what to do. We had you in mind and hope that with some thoughtful reflection about your first year and some selected reading herein you'll know better where to take charge (even how) and when and where to let your organization move and evolve in ways that are natural.

Or perhaps you were elected (well, no ballots or primaries and maybe not even any competition) to be board president a few months back and now after a few board meetings you are beginning to understand what it is really like. We had you in mind and hope that a thing or two on these pages will help you take hold of this curious job and make the organization better and your job even more satisfying.

Or possibly you agreed to be president-elect and know that you have exactly one swift year to figure out how to be a good president. There don't seem to be a lot of stellar examples around and mostly you decide you'll figure it out when you get there. We had you in mind and hope that if you watch closely what goes on (and doesn't) and read a few pages here and there, you'll feel a whole lot more ready to do the half dozen or so things most important for success.

Whatever your particular situation, your board and you, as their leader, have been entrusted with a mission that not so many years ago caused enough enthusiasm for a small group to care deeply enough to wade through state and federal forms and become incorporated and tax exempt. With some luck, part of what they believed in is still alive and well today and in need of your careful tending. And with any luck at all it is still important enough — valuable enough in your community that it is worthy of your attention. In short, it is now up to you — not primarily someone you hire — to receive this mission, recapture the initial enthusiasm, and hold in safe keeping all that is best and most crucial about this organization for the people in your community.

Those lines might lead you to believe that we think being a board president is no small matter, nothing to be done only in ceremonial fashion. That would be right and now you deserve to know who the "we" are that are so convinced about the importance of the board presidency.

The basics — our names and what we do in real life — are on the back cover where you would expect. Together the six of us have had over 36 years experience as board presidents and frankly not all of that quite wonderful. We have tried and sometimes even succeeded at being good board presidents of organizations with budgets both small and large. In human services, education, health, religious community organizations, and the arts we have attempted to hold in trust missions directed at performing music, rebuilding center cities, enhancing family life, educating children and youth, eliminating disease and organizing for better police protection. While we have in common being over 49, we live in the center city, suburbs, and small towns, are not only ethnically diverse but tend to be fairly colorful and outspoken characters. We fully discovered that on a two-day retreat where we talked about what we had learned being board presidents ourselves and observing many more, and as we debated what was worth sharing with you. We have left the writing down of it all to a colleague who, while himself at times a board president, has spent his career as an executive director. To maintain the balance, one of us is the editor and all of us have debated and refined the words on these pages. Perhaps this is enough to let you know about the collective "we."

A word about these pages. While we presumed to call this a book it is mercifully short. Two reasons. Our experience is that board presidents are busy people, and there are not 101 crucial things to say about being board president. We have tried to stick to essentials and share what we know briefly. We also begin with what we won't be saying much about, either because it is self-evident or said better elsewhere. We decided that there are a few essentials that we just could not skip over, and so we have short chapters on planning and evaluation, fundraising, board and staff roles, and the special relationship between the president and the executive. Those come first under Part Two: The Expected Essentials. In Part Three: Some Unexpected Essentials we move to five less expected areas that we have found to be crucial in the role of president. These you can and should do something about. In order those chapters are: The Year-Round Nominating Committee, Hearing Things: The Many Voices of the Board, Choreographing the Board Meeting, Discovering Your Leadership Voice, An Ethic of Authenticity, and Presidential Vigilance.

Our experience tells us that if you pay careful attention to nine things you will likely be an effective board president. Trying to pay close attention to twenty-three things can scatter your energy and cause your board to lose focus. On the other hand, concentrating on two or three things can allow some really important aspects of your organization to slip and quickly spin out of control. Nine may not be exactly the magic number but it isn't far off. Try it and let us know.

A final preliminary. We'd like to urge you not to go cover to cover here as though each small chapter will be equally important to you. While the sequence does have a certain rationality, chapter five is not dependent upon your reading chapter four. So scan the index, leaf through, start your mental conversation with us wherever it works best for you. You are in charge of this interchange just as you must be thoughtfully in charge of leading your organization. Do have a good and satisfying time of it. We would prefer being there with you, but for now, being there on these pages is the best we can do.

And do remember that as board president, what you do and how you do it is crucial far beyond the life of your organization. Robert Greenleaf, a wise and trusted writer, says it this way, "There is no other way that as few people can raise the quality of the whole American society as far and as fast as can trustees of our voluntary institutions, using the strength they now have in the positions they now hold."

We wish you success and satisfaction in building and using that strength.

Chapter 2

Good Common Sense

W hile common sense is always good, some would say it's not so common these days. Having said that, for some of you what follows will be evident, even elementary. So move on. But others may appreciate a quick review peppered with some of our experiences at trying to make things go well in a variety of organizations. Do feel entirely free to pick and choose from among these items those that remind you of something that as board president you don't want to forget.

WHAT WE HAVE LEARNED...

Beware of Norms and Formulas

Too much of what we have read about boards and board leadership stresses the way everyone "ought to" organize and function. It is as though somewhere out there is the perfect pattern or mold that we all should emulate. The fact is there are very few things that you absolutely must do as a board and a very great number that you can invent for your particular situation and the special people who serve with you in positions of leadership. We greatly favor putting you and your fellow board members in charge of determining the "what works best for us" question rather than urging you to follow the dictates of an organizational rulebook.

What we think is most exciting about being a board president is the latitude you have to lead your colleagues to create and recreate the kind of board and organization you wish to have. You can have a board of five or fifty. You can meet twelve times a year or three. You can have all the staff sit in on your meetings or none but the executive. You can have board member evaluations, sit in on staff meetings, meet individually with board members, or have those with whom you work attend board meetings and tell the board firsthand about that experience. You can even start every meeting with a reading from an article that pertains to your work or end every meeting with good news reports about your programs. The point is that you can and should take hold of the culture of the place — the way things are done, the way decisions are made, the way people are treated — and with your colleagues create a distinctive place that gives a special organizational character to all you do.

So you will find that in what follows there is a distinct absence of "always" and "never." Except in matters like truth and theft, the dogmatic qualifiers of always and never have little place in organizational life. What precise set of skills board presidents must always have, what community sectors board members should always represent, what roles, paid or unpaid, leaders should never perform seem to us less and less clear the more we are acquainted with the rich and complex variety and size of organizations in the not-for-profit sector. If someone asks if a board member should be involved in programming or if an executive should assist with investment policy the answer must certainly be "it depends." It depends on the people but most importantly it depends on the kind of organization you wish to have.

And so in what follows, while we ask you to consider focusing on nine issues, we urge you to entertain various responses to those issues that match up with who you wish to be as a board president and what you and your colleagues wish to shape as your own distinctive organizational culture.

Prepare the Way for Accomplishment

The "we just sit around and discuss" and "we never seem to get anything done" complaints are signs of ineffective board leadership. An obvious and crucial part of your job as board president is to create the environment, the systems, and the structure so that work is accomplished, talk leads to action, and plans take shape in reality. Some boards have committee reports that focus only on actions taken. Other board presidents couch their own reports to the board in terms of "here's what has been accomplished since we last met." Board members tend to respond and wish to become more involved when there is an atmosphere of accomplishment. They not surprisingly like to give their time when things happen and the organization advances. For boards of trustees, progress and forward movement are great rewards and motivators and you as board president must lead the way to see that things are in place for accomplishment.

Don't Let Anyone Mess Up the Deal

No doubt you've been in meetings where one person monopolizes in an aggressive fashion and makes honest give and take quite impossible. Some people seem able to bring whole organizations to a halt. By whatever combination of demands, criticism, or contrariness, they impede discussion and bring real organizational progress to a near stop. As board president, with or without assistance from the executive director, you need to find a way to keep that from happening. As leader of the board you must protect the whole board in its deliberations and processes from the disruptive tendencies of any one board member.

It very well may require a private conversation with the individual, and it might include eliciting the support of another board member. But, in whatever fashion, you have to find a way. Unfortunately, courtesy, often coupled in the phrase "common courtesy," is too often not so common and in some situations will not work. So draw on whatever combination of charm and authority you have so that no one person will mess up the deal.

No Surprises, Please...

One of our favorite board members addressing a room full of executive directors said, "I need only three things to join your board and the first is to promise me that there will be no surprises." This was not a control request to eliminate acts of God and foundation directors. This is, "Don't call me up after I've joined the board and tell me there is a two-hundred thousand dollar deficit." This is, "Don't introduce an agenda item at the end of the meeting that begins with the sentence, 'Last evening our lease was canceled.'" This is, "Don't tell me at the end of the fiscal year that all board members are expected to give one thousand dollars."

Yes, given the environment in which not-for-profits operate and given the complexity of organizational personalities the unexpected will surface. But in organizational life too much of what is unexpected is the result of not-so-good planning, less than smart projections, and simply not anticipating what could reasonably enough be anticipated. For a board to know in advance, to have all the information necessary, to face problems when they first occur is to have a board whose president is trusted and held in high regard. No surprises, please.

Be Open To Explore Collaborations

There are at least two misperceptions about not-for-profit organizations that would be useful for you to counteract. One is that there are just too many organizations who do essentially the same thing asking for money. And two is that not-for-profits are very territorial and not inclined to cooperate with one another. No one knows what the optimum number of not-for-profits of one kind or another really is any more than the optimum number of drug stores or gas stations. What we do know is that for not-for-profits to have a spirit of cooperation is a healthy thing and probably in a self-interested way is likely to increase your base of clients or your size of audience. So for whatever mix of reasons be a board president who is always asking, "Is there someone else in town we should talk to about doing this new proposal jointly?" or "Is there anyone who already does after school programs or midweek concerts or Saturday schools with whom we could partner?"

True collaborations — partnerships in something old or new — are not easy and the costs need to be carefully measured. Costs in this case are not merely money but staff and volunteer time and the energy required to weld two different organizational cultures into doing one thing well. But as an attitude, as a citizen of the community, board presidents need to lead the way in asking and acting on collaboration in a way that models openness and a sense of the big picture.

There Is Unavoidable Discomfort in Doing Things Well

This is something like one board president we know saying, "you are probably not taking on big enough challenges if it is all going smoothly." An absence of stress, resistance, unease may be a sign that you are not leading strongly enough, not addressing what needs attention, not going for a level of excellence that will make you and your board proud. While this is not a statement in celebration of stress, since much stress comes from bad leadership, it is an acknowledgement that if you move to change the way meetings are conducted or try to have a thoughtful evaluation of your executive or ask for the evidence that your marketing program is going well, you will be stirring the organization pot in some ways that will cause discomfort. We happen to believe it is the kind of discomfort that necessarily will come in the pursuit of doing better as an organization.

About Finance

Don't assume that otherwise smart board members know how to read your organization's financial report. This very well might be a good opportunity for you and the board treasurer to do some orientation and training. You can always use the "need to brief new board members" as an excuse, or even blame the peculiar way you do your financial statements. (Incidentally, peculiar may be just fine for your size budget, but you may want to call for a review of the format that you use.) For the sake of clarity and simplicity, you may even wish to propose some changes.

All board members deserve to know at least quarterly the status of income based on budget projections, the amount and kind of expenses compared to the budget, and the total amount of funds available in all accounts. That information is basic for a financial report and it needs to be regularly and dependably presented in understandable fashion so that all board members get it, especially those who claim not to "do numbers."

As for audits, sometimes they are expensive, but almost always they are necessary. If your organization has a budget of under $250,000 the board may opt to have audits done on an every other year basis.

Finally, while you are in charge of seeing that all of the above happens with regard to finance, make sure that the board treasurer is involved, as well as the staff person responsible for finance. And put a budget review on the agenda at every board meeting.

About Liability

Don't be frightened into potentially expensive directors' liability policies until you know the facts and can reasonably calculate your risk.

Another mistake would be to assume that if restitutional or punitive damages have to be paid as a result of legal action or administrative decision the full cost will be borne by the institution, saving the board and its individual members from any liability.

While your state attorney general's office is likely to have up-to-date information about transfer liability, Cyril Hoube, writing in *Governing Boards,* outlines five important guidelines related to risk protection. The following is a synopsis of each:

1. Most states provide for the indemnification of board members. You should check the exact provision in this regard under the laws of your state.

2. State laws that apply to not-for-profit corporations provide guidelines concerning actions permissible on the part of boards. Some board member should be aware of these provisions and be prepared to monitor their application.

3. The board should make a conscious decision about how much directors' and officers' insurance it needs, what sort and how much it is willing to pay.

4. Boards must exercise care in protecting themselves against board actions that might lead to fiscal liability. Pay particular attention to self-interested decisions, payroll taxes, and fraud and deal with them quickly and forthrightly. Also of importance are problems related to mismanagement, dereliction of duty, and the offering of impermissible programs.

5. The board should establish checks on performance and reporting procedures that will likely reveal early detection of troubling issues.

If this all seems too complicated or burdensome seek the advice of someone in your state attorney general's office or consult a trusted attorney.

About Conflict of Interest

Oftentimes the issues here are very clear. In simple terms you need to ask the question, "Are there ways in which we function as an organization that result in undue and inappropriate benefit to board members, staff or constituents?" Specifically is there:

- Undue constituent influence
- Undue financial benefit to board members
- Unfair bidding and contracting practices involving board members or friends
- Personal or intimate relationships within the organization that jeopardize fair decision making

In short, as board president you need to be aware of the policies and practices of your organization to see that no unfair advantage or undue benefit may occur.

About Bylaws

Most of the time you'll inherit them, not have to create them. Unfortunately too much of the time it will be difficult to locate a copy. That will give you some clue about their importance in your organization. Early in your presidency or even before you assume the leadership, you should know what they say. You should also understand what it takes to revise or suspend them. (Generally, two-thirds vote of the board.) And if they seem too restrictive or no longer appropriate, identify some board members who appreciate both detail and simplicity and produce a revision for board approval.

Pay particular attention to those sections of the by-laws that deal with board membership. How are potential board members identified? How are they elected? For what term of office? May they be reelected and on what grounds may they be removed? Generally, bylaws with flexibility are most workable when they contain phrases such as, "up to 24 board members," "up to ten meetings a year," and "there shall be an executive committee and whatever program and administrative committees that from time to time seem important and necessary."

Get sample by-laws from other organizations about your size whom you respect. Don't make a by-law revision process the centerpiece of several board meetings. In our experience, by-laws are most important when they enable you to do the administrative and programmatic work you need to do with a maximum of efficiency and ease.

Part II

Experiencing the Expected Essentials

Chapter 3

Planning

You will not be surprised that we begin by drawing your attention to five items which you have already figured out will command your energies: planning, fundraising, evaluation, the board and staff partnership, and your own special relationship with the organization's executive. Upon these five you must fix your most creative and thoughtful attention. Our own experience tells us if these basics are nicely in place you are likely to be regarded and remembered as a fine board president. At first they may seem a bit common and ordinary. We will try to talk with you about these in ways that allow you to see them with fresh eyes and approach them with a sense of new enthusiasm. They are, after all, the heart and soul of organizational life and deserve to be treated with great care and imagination. Let's try.

The captain of the ship metaphor may not be exactly right for you as board president but you do need to do some steering. While we aren't sure we entirely buy George Bernard Shaw's comment, "To be in hell is to drift, to be in heaven is to steer," we do acknowledge that drifting is what happens in an organization where the planning function is not done well. You as president need to see that there is a thoughtful planning process and more importantly a habit of planning.

The need to plan may sneak up on you in a variety of ways. As you are reading the new funding guidelines for your local United Way, arts agency, or community foundation, you might run into the bold-face type, "Every organization requesting funds must provide a three-year strategic plan." That makes it fairly unavoidable. Or it could just be that your organization has a history of writing a plan every three years and though it seems only months since the last planning process ended, it truly is time to begin again.

The impetus for "doing a plan" may also come from a budget crisis, personnel problem, split in the board, or just general malaise and search for something useful to do. For whatever reason it pops up on your organizational agenda, planning is largely unavoidable, often surprisingly useful, and usually able to be accomplished successfully without a three-day retreat, a high-priced consultant, or an exhausted and grumpy board.

The problem often is just getting started. And getting started is not an easy matter because there is a lot of mystique and jargon around planning and a lot of healthy (and not so healthy) resistance to taking the time to do it.

When you as board president prepare to help the whole board see the value of planning, that mystique and jargon will be a stumbling block. An expected response may be "we tried that several years ago and it didn't work." Likely, at that time, the timing, process, personnel involved (all or some) conspired to make it a less-than-productive experience — which means yet another challenge and reason to explore and patiently discuss planning with the full board. No doubt you and others on your board have had a mix of good and bad organizational planning experiences.

Rather than trying to sell planning as a pure and perfect enterprise, engaging in an open discussion among the partners regarding ambiguities and merits of planning more likely will lead to acceptance.

Perhaps the most perplexing issue to surface during such discussions is the delicate balance between action and planning. Funds do need to be raised and services do need to be provided; both crucial activities require time and energy. Planning is often squeezed out by the imperatives of action, forward motion and financial need.

There is an "action bias" in many organizations and perhaps in all of us who have to produce events and services and to make our organizations work. There may even be an anti-planning bias in the leadership and membership of not-for-profit organizations who see the mission as so big, the real need so great that "we simply must get on with it and not talk about it." That's all real and needs to be acknowledged, as do the often bad experiences with organizational planning that have been too long, too costly, and too beside the point. And yet a failure to plan can deprive the organization of insights into new opportunities, cost-saving efficiencies, establishing measurable performance criteria, and jettisoning outmoded practices.

Let's look at three basic questions for you to explore as you bring your full board (and perhaps others) to a thoughtful planning process that works with your organization's particular configuration of issues, people, and history.

THREE QUESTIONS
BEFORE YOU BEGIN

As you think of your full board being involved in a planning activity, perhaps a two-day retreat won't fit into their schedules. And while three or four evenings spaced over six to eight weeks might seem more palatable, attendance would be sixty to seventy-five percent with those absent including people whose contribution you don't want to miss.

Most boards today will not sit still for leisurely planning no matter how crucial the need or how well-organized the process. So while "compression planning" has unfortunate connotations, focusing intently for a short period of time with a well-organized process is probably the best guide for the organizational culture of the new century.

To put it more radically, if there are a maximum of eight precious organizational leadership hours available for planning, four might well be used by a small group getting ready so that the four left will be highly productive and satisfying for the whole board.

The following check list of questions can be used by you and the executive in the crucial first half of the overall planning effort:

1. "Why are you spending time planning?"

You want to be able to better track and evaluate your product. This will push you toward planning oriented around program and services and incorporating quantifiable measures.

You have to comply with the mandate of a funder or super agency. The question here is whether you merely comply and get it done and out of the way. If so, make sure you are clear not only about what must be included but also about who must be included to meet the established guidelines. If you decide to use the necessity of producing a plan as an opportunity to address some of your own important issues, then determine what they are and how they fit into the mandated planning process.

You are motivated by a current or impending financial crisis. Of course, attend to all the numbers, the relative cost and benefit of things, the use of part-time and volunteer personnel. But don't give in to long-term dominance by the finance committee. Among all the important financial questions must be the "what do we really care about doing" question. This focus on mission should help develop both programmatic and funding solutions together.

Your board, staff, and members are tired, uninspired, even bored. This happens in the life of organizations. The condition need not be disastrous and is an excellent motivation for a planning process. The orientation for this effort is less on detail, outcomes, and strategies and more on recapturing the original enthusiasm that gave birth to the organization, or the present enthusiasms that reside in those key to the life of the organization.

2. "Who should do this planning?"

Most everyone would agree that you as president together with the executive ought to initiate and be in on the planning. At a minimum, you will also probably want to include the officers and/or the full executive committee and possibly two or more past presidents. Don't forget clients and would-be clients so your organization avoids planning in isolation. Beyond that, it is your call based on the reason for the planning process and the amount of time your organization can apply to it. In making that decision, consider these models, termed "largely inclusive," "carefully selective," and "strategically external." Explanations follow.

Largely inclusive: This involves the organization's full board, professional staff, auxiliary or advisory boards, sub-committees, constituent groups, and past presidents. This method has the advantage of attending to all and overlooking no one and, therefore, may be what is needed if there have been problems and lack of open communication. But it is cumbersome and challenging to manage this method efficiently.

One variation is to involve the many participants in different ways. Some may be interviewed by phone or in person. Some may respond to a written form with open-ended questions and check lists of items for ranking. All need not be in the room hammering out the plan but all would be there at the beginning (expressing concerns and hopes) and the end (responding to a final draft). This model is more complex and may be more successful with outside consultation and coordination.

Carefully selective: This approach uses key players and requires careful consideration of just who should participate. Easiest of all is to involve the executive and the executive committee. Beyond that, you must be able to explain to the rest of the organization why you are selecting specific additional people and, by implication, not selecting others.

You might consider one or two additional senior staff members, a new board member or two, a past chair, someone from your membership or donor list who has recently shown enthusiasm for your efforts or someone whose involvement on the board or a sub-committee has decreased dramatically. The key is the right mix and that means including some who may resist change and may not be in the camp of the present leadership.

Strategically external: Developing a plan need not be only internal to the organization. There are many good reasons to include important people outside your organization. These people need not all participate at the same level and in the same way. They may respond in interviews, focus groups, or questionnaires, or they may react to draft documents.

You can best determine who to include. For some it will be consumers or clients, and for others, major funders, government agencies, or appointing authorities. You might consider potential (or actual) collaborators, representatives of parallel agencies in other communities, faculty and researchers, media representatives, and specific ethnic groups presently under-represented in your organization.

Involving outsiders often is not a neat, tidy, or comfortable experience. It may, however, be the creative disruption your organization needs to recapture its energy and distinctiveness.

3. "Is there such a thing as a good time to plan?"

Unless you have an entirely astrological approach to life, there is probably no perfect time to initiate a planning process. The question is one of readiness. When are you most likely to get the best attention of the people you want to have participate? The following list presents planning time determined by some organizations to be right:

- *Just before a new fiscal year* — Budgetary decisions are made at this time and it may also be opportune to ask about broader organizational issues.

- *When you are about to select a new executive director or new board members* — In either case leadership selection decisions can be better informed if they are influenced by a thoughtful organizational planning process.

- *At the time you install new officers or a new executive director* — A time of leadership change presents enough of a hitch in the usual way of doing business that it is often an opportunity for reflection and planning.

- *When there is a specific problem* — A specific problem is different from a general crisis. The problem may be clearer and its resolution more effective if addressed in the broader context of an overall planning process.

- *If your organizational environment is disrupted* — A disruption may be a new competitor, a change in funding guidelines, a political or economic change in your community, or something else. In any case, it requires taking stock and responding, and may be a good occasion for planning.

- *Before launching a new venture* — The opportunity for planning may occur as you decide whether or not to launch a new venture or during the launch itself. In either case, there will be an impact on the organization which may cause you to think more broadly about organizational plans and purposes.

- *As an ongoing process* — This is not a periodic work stoppage for planning. It is more an attitude of forethought, a disposition to reflect and project the possibilities and consequences of various directions and actions.

THE PLANNING PROCESS: THREE MODELS

Getting where you want to go and allowing for side trips is not just a family vacation dilemma. Organizational life is a constant balancing act between the destination-bound and the side trippers, between the importance of staying focused and on track and the equal importance of experimenting and opening up new territory. Good planning equips an organization for both, and good leadership partners insist on the co-existence of directness and diversion.

The planning process itself needs to be well-focused and tightly organized with equal amounts of creativity and humor. As you devise your own planning process from the three models which follow, don't forget the focused part or the fun part. And as you live out the life of your plan, stay on track but don't miss anything of delightful import along the way.

One final note. There seems to be more than enough written about management objectives, quantifiable goals and detailed month-by-month plans. Instead, we have chosen to focus on three different levels of planning. They do have in common the assumption that your basic mission is fairly well established and your products and services mostly determined. We hope that at least one of the planning modes might assist you in the planning necessary to enliven or redirect your organization.

The three modes that follow in summary fashion are: planning as an agenda for action, planning as an organizational tonic, and planning as commitment to guidelines.

1. Planning as an Agenda for Action
(or "How to avoid saddling up and riding off in all directions")

In Summary

Focus:	Specific organizational and programmatic accomplishment
Planning period:	One to two years
Participants:	15–25 people (or a number you feel okay about working together in one group)
Time required:	Four to six hours for full group, four to six hours in preparation by a leadership group of three to five
Advantages:	Is relatively quick, focuses on tangible items, forges a consensus, pays attention to what we want to do versus what we should do or historically have done, or what might be interesting
Disadvantages:	Requires quick decision making that may be uncomfortable for those who work best with more reflection; also may cause concern among those uncomfortable with a "let's just try it for a year or so" attitude

---

This is an agenda for action planning — quick, non-detailed, focused on the present energy of the board and oriented around doing. It may be worth thinking about and worth trying in some form for a year.

2. Planning as an Organizational Tonic
(or "Rx for boredom, the blues, and the blahs.")

Tonic used to be more associated with spring than gin. Most organizations can use the rejuvenating effects of a spring tonic from time to time. Since good planning ought to result not merely in efficient implementation but in implementation characterized by vigor, even passion, attention to the fire that drives the engine is altogether an appropriate planning activity.

This approach is not precisely aimed at what your organization should do or when or how. It is directed at assisting the organizational leadership to connect and reconnect with the initial dream, enthusiasm or fire that gave birth to your agency. Such a return to the beginnings will focus and revitalize the efforts of your organization. Any good planning activity should do the same.

In Summary

Focus:	The essential enthusiasm that initiated the organization, the continuing enthusiasms that drive the present leadership
Planning period:	One year
Participants:	The board
Time required:	Two hours of reflective time
Advantages:	The strength is in re-focusing, re-energizing and re-committing board leadership.
Disadvantages:	This method will not deliver specifics but will provide a livelier context in which decisions about specific objectives will be easier and better made.

Setting and mood are crucial for this conversation. It might get done well in one and a half hours. It won't get done if your board is feeling plagued by pressing decisions or the execution of business details. Board members who tend to be fairly task oriented may need a rationale for "this much time spent just philosophizing." A reasonable rationale goes something like, "We always seem to have too much to do and often find ourselves spending efforts on activities not central to what we are about. Today we are going to work to clarify that essential purpose so we make better decisions about time and resources." Or, "We seem to use a lot of energy on the structures and procedures we have devised to carry out what it is we really are about. Let's make sure we remember what this is and give that special enthusiasm more attention."

3. Planning as Commitment to Guidelines

(or "How to avoid the 'set aside your principles and do what's right' approach to organizational life.")

We've looked at creating a specific agenda for action and attempting to recapture and refocus organizational enthusiasms. This model falls between specific tasks and broad purposes. The issue is not, "what exactly shall we do" or "what do we care deeply about." Rather, "what are the guidelines that grow naturally from what we care about and therefore determine what we will do."

Further, this model is entirely comprehensive. All aspects of the organization will be subject to your carefully crafted guidelines which will serve as precise indicators for decision and action. While it is entirely possible (perhaps even useful) to apply this model only to fund development or programming, we will proceed as though you may want to apply it to the whole life of your organization.

In Summary

Focus: Establishing clear guidelines for decision-making and action in all aspects of the organization

Planning period: One to three years

Participants: Full board, perhaps with subcommittee representation

Time required: 1 to 1-1/2 hours for each component of your organization; you may do them one at a time over a year.

Advantages: Touches everything in the life of the organization, creates benchmarks that will assist greatly in future decisions.

Disadvantages: Can become tedious and time consuming and may unnecessarily delay or derail timely action on crucial issues.

The key question to be asked in a variety of ways is what are the guiding principles that should determine our action, whether in marketing or building a budget. Work to avoid simplistic ethics (honesty, loyalty). Also avoid action-level statements about "how we really ought to do this."

A budget-building guideline might be "board and staff representatives from each program area will make the initial recommendations about the budget for the new year." A guideline that is too general and therefore not as useful is "the budget must always reflect our values." A too specific and therefore controlling guideline is "each new budget will not vary from the previous year's budget by more than five percent."

To determine how to build your own guidelines, it might help to look at your organization in two ways around categories that work best in your situation. The first is by departments or divisions (generally a delineation of activity around which most boards build subcommittees). The second is by process functions, aspects of organization management that occur in human resources as well as program and services. Remember that in each case you are looking for clear statements that guide, not for beliefs or courses of action.

With luck and large doses of persistence and imagination, you will be able to steer the board through a satisfying planning process. However, everyone needs to be reminded that planning probably is most powerfully construed as an attitude rather than an occasion. Of course, occasionally you will want to take a pause in your hectic organizational life for an intentional planning process. But your enterprise likely will be more vital, more on target if the planning attitude regularly permeates your activity. The best planning questions, the most thoughtful planning processes rather than being securely stored away for once-a-year planning ought to be encouraged to pop up in the middle of a board meeting, executive evaluation, or a discussion about new officers.

We urge you to develop your own best planning attitude that puts reflection in the middle of action and drops big questions in the middle of small tactics. Use whatever bits and pieces from this section that work best for you. Fashion a plan that you can feel positive about infusing into the life of your organization. And don't forget the good questions you asked and the thoughtful discussions you had to get there. They are worth remembering, learning and repeating. That's the planning attitude indicative of healthy organizations.

Chapter 4

Fundraising

The proper spirit of all this money chasing business is best captured by Booker T. Washington and his experience of trying to raise money in the early days of the Tuskegee Institute. He wrote in *Up From Slavery*, "While the work of going from door to door and office to office is hard, disagreeable and costly in bodily strength, it has some compensations. Such work gives one a rare opportunity to study human nature. It also has its compensations in giving one the opportunity to meet some of the best people in the world — to be more correct, I think I should say the best people in the world. When one takes a broad survey of the country you will find that the most useful and influential people in it are those that take the deepest interest in institutions that exist for the purpose of making the world better."

Now we are guessing that you have agreed to be board president because you believe your organization can make the world a better place. Believing that and talking with others about supporting your organization will, in fact, lead you to meet fine people, generous people who, like you, want to feel a part of organizations that help make life fuller and better in your part of the world. That's the inspiring part.

The more daunting part is finding ways to raise all the money you need to do what is so important. Here are some ways for you to think about and act on the task of creating revenue for your organization. First of course you don't approach this task with a clean slate. There are lots of things in place. Whether your budget is $200,000 or $2 million, one way or another much of that money has been coming through the door and, with luck, much of it dependably. You probably have inherited a committee who does part of it, a staff person or two who do another part, and maybe an auxiliary or friends group that does yet another part. You need to understand all that well and listen for how and why it goes smoothly and how and why it is a bit rough. It might be good to convene the five or ten people who make it work and talk all about how and why it does or doesn't work.

THREE WAYS TO CREATE REVENUE

At least for your own thinking about the big picture of creating revenue, here's a way to think about it that may help get your arms around this crucial and complex task.

Try thinking of all the ways that funds come in to your organization in three broad categories: Products, Philanthropy, and Ploys. After explaining what each of these includes, we'll attempt some percent of total income suggestions you may want to assign to each and finally offer our own sense about the advantages and disadvantages of the methods of raising funds presented in each of the three categories.

Products are anything you do as part of your mission from which income is derived. They may be tangible things or they may be services. Most often your "products" bring in fees, admissions, sales, or dues. Philanthropy (and we understand this is not literally correct) generates revenue in support of the work you do rather than for products or services you produce. This would include money received from individuals, foundations, corporations, and government agencies. Ploys bring in funds as a result of efforts other than the work of your mission. This would include a great number of events such as special events, raffles, auctions (silent and noisy), golf outings, and tennis matches.

There you have it in total. Not a perfect system. A bit of overlap here and there but perhaps a fresh way to grasp all the activity that goes into the creation of revenue for your organization. Now let's look a little deeper at each of the three categories.

Products

The products of your organization, whether classes, counseling, or concerts, are a legitimate part of your revenue creation endeavor. While they are not usually thought of as fundraising, they in fact raise funds for your organization and we find it useful to think of them as part of the total effort toward providing necessary income. We have heard some board members say that they have a goal of creating 50% of their annual income from the work of the organization. That may be low. We know of one science museum that for years received 90% of its budget from admissions. We know of a historic preservation district that receives over 90% of its total income from lease arrangements. When the work that flows from your mission creates a large portion of your revenue there is a desirable economy of effort within your organization. If, on the other hand, you have to do the work of your mission and rely on doing the work of fund development by other means, that, of course, requires more of everyone, often more employees or volunteers.

Back to the 50% goal for products. It may be too high. If you are doing job readiness and placement services with out-of-school youth you may be in that barren financial field where clients can't pay and the government won't write contracts. Serving those who do not have the personal resources to pay does not, however, mean no income from services. Oftentimes a third party, usually local or state government, will provide funds on a fee for contract basis. In any case, funds which come to your organization because of the work you do enable you to focus both your programmatic and fund creation efforts in the same activity. That is a good place to be.

Philanthropy

As you strive to generate revenue in support of what you do, be mindful that most of it will come from individuals. Generally individuals come to support your organization in one of three ways: they give through an annual fund, they give to support or sponsor a specific activity or program, or they participate in planned giving. All these require staff and often board members' time and attention to build relationships and, in the case of planned giving, may require special information or assistance.

An annual fund we know about raises 10% of the organization's budget (about $60,000). What they do is send out about 4,000 letters in October with a form on which are giving levels of $40 to over $5,000. The letter is personal and tells the story of the work they do. It is short, colorful, and reminds those who receive it that this is a once-a-year request. About 300 families respond and then a follow-up post card is sent early in December to a select group of 1,500. Another 100 or so respond to this request. The cost is about $1,800 for the two mailings' printing, postage, and mailing service. The executive director spends about four to five hours writing the two requests. Support staff donate another four hours to organize the lists and printed materials and get them to the printer and mailing service. You don't need a very sharp pencil to compute that spending $1,800 cash and about 8 hours of staff time to raise $60,000 is a good return.

There are three or four points to underline from this story. First, it requires that your organization create and maintain a mailing list of people who care about your work. Second, it is yet more effective if board members write personal notes on letters to selected individuals. And third, if you do say it is a once-a-year request, guarantee that is the case and make it happen once a year at the same time so it will be expected. Finally, not in the story as first told is the fact that this organization has a small core of volunteers who send out thank you notes on post cards, handwritten and signed. A little hard to do and organize but a big boost to repeat giving, and if done promptly, a memorable touch unfortunately done by too few.

In terms of a combination of cash and return on investment, it doesn't get much better than that annual letter illustration. But there are in almost every community individuals capable of giving in excess of $10,000 who genuinely care about the work you do. Usually this requires no cash expenditure but rather requires considerable time to identify and cultivate these friends. People give to people. Potential donors must get to know and trust you — some say six contacts before an ask. Again, this requires staff planning and execution. The larger the organization the more detailed, time consuming, and expensive the task. Board members have a role here: seeing that it's done to begin with and then helping to cultivate the best prospects.

Planned giving is also a form of philanthropy. On this subject there are books and consultants and no small detail. In short you should explore it. It will not produce revenue until well into the future and in all cases must be handled on a very personal basis. One organization started with its board and rather quickly got 25% of its members (that would be 6) to name the organization in their will or in a fund at the local community foundation. Then those few members talked about what they had done to a few more long-time supporters. At best it is a slow and mostly quiet process and likely to be worth the effort it will take. And again, the larger the organization, the larger the effort.

As president you will probably need some direct involvement in individual giving and will also need to be involved in pursuing corporations for donations and sponsorships. There is not much magic here. Most corporations will sponsor events or programs where they receive substantial name recognition. They of course are more apt to be interested where their own customers or employees are involved or where their services or products relate in some positive way to your services and products. We probably need not remind you that they may also be willing to give away their services (attorneys, accountants) or the products they produce or sell (computers, desks). Here the expenditure is again more time than money. And the time is related to the slow, careful process of building relationships and writing good letters and reports.

Speaking of writing, grant writing can provide substantial revenue to an organization. As president you should be sure your organization has explored the possibilities. Mostly this will be through foundations and government agencies and often times the writing involves extensive forms and attachments that require anywhere from 20 to 80 hours of work. Two small hints: Don't overestimate the technique of proposal writing and don't underestimate the importance of pre-proposal talking and corresponding. Your grants writer should be able to think clearly and write well. If your staff is sending out blind proposals, like sending out blind resumes for jobs, it mostly doesn't work. As a rule, the likelihood of funding and the amount can be determined up front if you spend thoughtful time with foundation program officers. Obviously spending extensive time where there is at least a 50-50 chance of a positive response is what you want your organization to be doing.

Ploys

Ploys we put last because in order of what you should be doing and assisting others to do, that is where they belong. If most of the time can be spent focusing on obtaining funds from the admissions, fees, and sales that result from the programs and projects of your organization, that will save time and money. If another significant amount of income can come from those individuals, foundations, government agencies, and corporations who have one reason or another to care about what you are doing, that is good as well. If you must create ploys to convince people who care more about those ploys than the work of your organization to give you their money, that may prove to be necessary but it isn't greatly desirable. There is nothing inherently wrong with special events, auctions, and golf outings, but they do run three risks. One is that you will become better known for the ploy than for your organization and its mission. Second, you may exhaust staff and/or volunteers on this non-mission related activity. Third, you will end up with sizable income but likewise sizable expense and, therefore, very little net positive result. If you can create a ploy that sounds like your mission, does not take hundreds of hours of staff and volunteer time, and brings you substantial net income, then it just may be worth doing.

We offer the following percentages of income based on our own experience, realizing that you may have a very special situation that will call for a different plan.

Products (admissions, fees, sales) 40-60% of income. Philanthropy (individuals, foundations, corporations) 30-40% of income. Ploys (special events, auctions, raffles) 10-20% of income.

In any case, these suggested percentages can form the basis for a thoughtful conversation among the board, executive, and those in your organization responsible for bringing in the income. Then you can decide together what works for your organization and exactly what kind of a fund development system you wish to have for your organization.

Chapter 5

Evaluation

Most would agree that evaluation is key to improving any organization. However, few would agree that it is carried out in a way that excites or inspires. All of us have seen the benefits of evaluations done well and the frustrations and casualties from those done poorly. And we are convinced that both programmatic and board evaluations are important. But to keep our effort here relatively lively, simple, and focused, we have chosen not to talk about programmatic evaluation, although we encourage you to check with other resources for guidance. Rather, we will attend to the work, participation, and satisfaction of the board.

Evaluating — actually reviewing and assessing the board — is what we are up to here, and we don't propose it in order to rate or give grades. It is all in the service of learning, of doing better. Our thought is that if you as board president set a tone for open and candid assessment of how things are going and how they could go better, that just may infect, even affect the whole of the organization. Give it a try and see what happens. What follows are some ideas, processes, and forms that may help.

Frankly speaking, there is nothing like a thorough-going organizational catastrophe to motivate a good board evaluation. A brand new executive can make it happen, or even a new president or a revered departing one. Sometimes a highly enough paid consultant from a far-away place can force the issue. Otherwise, it is tough. Board evaluation is too often viewed as unnecessary, embarrassing, or at least an interruption of the "real thing we are here for"— doing the business of the organization.

When should you do board evaluation? Perhaps at a year-end meeting, an annual retreat, or at the beginning of the year for mid-year implementation.

The notion of offering a choice may garner acceptance if not something near enthusiasm. In outline form, here are three ways of going about board evaluations:

1. Reviewing the work of the board: A list of primary board functions for discussion directed at balance and effectiveness.

2. Assessing board member satisfaction: Paying attention to the mix of personal rewards important to any group of board members.

3. Surveying board member participation: The level and kind of involvement of individual members.

There is enough for your board to make a choice or combine elements of each. Now we offer some direction about how to do each in a productive fashion.

1. Reviewing the Work of the Board

The full range of all that a board does is impressive to overwhelming. This experience will center on a few major and common tasks on the agenda of most boards. The purpose is not to assign a rank to "how we did in each." Instead, review all the items as a reminder of the breadth of activity and select three or four to concentrate on for the coming six months to a year. Specify what "concentrate on" means. What more or different do you want to do about item two or item seven? Who will be responsible to see that it gets done? In short, the full board should decide on the items, suggest goals pertaining to them, establish who will be responsible, and identify a time to review the progress.

This is not the whole world catalogue of board tasks and responsibilities. But it does encompass enough of the major ones for your board to settle on three or four that need concentrated attention.

2. Surveying Board Member Participation

This may work best in the form of an outline completed by individual board members and then discussed individually with the board president or chair of the nominating committee. The direction is toward assisting board members not only to be more involved, but also to be more appropriately involved.

These questions sent out to board members or used as part of a reflective time at a board meeting (and responses collected on the spot) may assist you in better utilizing the resources of your board membership.

Checklist of Potential Board Tasks

❏ Establish orientation procedures for new board members.

❏ Develop a way to create effective agendas for board meetings.

❏ Create a process for assisting the board to learn about current issues related to your organization's mission.

❏ Ensure the balance of detail work in committees and big issues work at board meetings.

❏ Explore ways of making more appropriate committee assignments and rotating committee chairs and members.

❏ Design an organizational planning process and a way to plan revision.

❏ Improve the developing and monitoring of the budgetary process.

❏ Enlarge the base of revenue support for the organization.

❏ Review the number and duration of board and committee meetings.

❏ Evaluate and encourage the executive.

❏ Forecast and prepare a succession plan.

❏ Recommend changes in the way key decisions are made within the organization.

❏ Re-evaluate core programs and services.

❏ Propose new strategies for marketing and public relations.

❏ Examine the sufficiency of existing personnel policies and procedures.

❏ Extend participation and collaboration with other organizations in your community.

Inventory of Board Member Participation

1. In the upcoming year on the board I would like to take personal responsibility for _____.

2. I would be willing to have further conversation about being considered for the following offices and committee chair positions:

        President   Secretary
        Vice President   Treasurer
        (List your committees)

3. My previous board involvement has been mostly _____.
I would like to move toward _____.

4. A new effort I think is important for our organization and that I would like to help with is _____.

5. A task I particularly enjoy at work that I have yet to do on this board is _____
_____.

6. My most treasured board experience has had to do with _____
_____.

7. I would consider this upcoming year a success if the board was able to _____.

3. Assessing Board Member Satisfaction

Most board members see themselves serving on the board as a matter of community service. They should also expect and receive personal satisfaction. Just as the organization is in business to have a positive impact on the lives of people in the community, that impact should extend to the lives of the board members themselves. The following questions will prompt attention to that concern and foster a conversation about the significance of the organization in the lives of the board members.

A Review of Board Member Satisfaction

1. What about this board makes you proud and eager to be a part of it?

2. What does the organization mean to your life?

3. How would your life be different if you were not part of this board?

4. What do your family and friends sense or believe about this organization by their association with you?

5. At what points in the work of this board do you feel best about yourself?

6. Yes, you are here to serve, but what do you get back, what keeps you happily involved?

This series of questions may work best not in writing but as a guided conversation at a retreat or part of a board meeting. It may take a bit of persistence to get some board members into a mode of identifying what personal satisfactions they are receiving. That, however, is the distinct tack of this evaluation experience. But do find ways to respond to what you hear. Asking and not responding is of course worse than not having asked at all.

In sum, the practice of board evaluation is likely a new one for your organization. Increasingly, not-for-profit organizations are experiencing the value of paying thoughtful attention to the exercise of board membership. Evaluation at its best can provide direction and motivation for the board leadership within your organization. It can, as well, assist in seeing that the leadership is more broadly shared and that future board leaders are being identified and prepared. For all those reasons, we believe board member evaluation is of real significance.

Chapter 6

Working Together: The Board and the Executive

Here is a big one. Our experience is that too quickly and too often boards and executives get at cross purposes and begin behaving as adversaries rather than colleagues. True, you as board president need to help the board in this "yes we hire and fire" and "yes we need to work as a team" balance with the executive. In the next chapter we will say more about your own special relationship with the executive. Here we address the who does what and why questions as they relate to board and executive.

Many of the problems among leaders in an organization result from the failure early on to be clear about who will do what (and maybe why). Much in the life of an organization can destroy working relationships, and most could be avoided if better understandings were in place. Some common misunderstandings include reaching unilateral decisions, taking actions without prior approval, exercising authority in a realm belonging to another, speaking on behalf of those who have not agreed to be spoken for, mixing policy making and program deciding, and committing funds or people without prior knowledge of the appropriate committee.

These common organizational problems result from the board and executive failing to plan thoughtfully, establish clear understandings, and maintain frequent and direct communication. If these are attended to, there will likely be a solid core of strength and effectiveness which will set the tone for the whole organization. In short, there are many good reasons to pay attention to the board-executive working relationship.

ESTABLISHING AN EFFECTIVE RELATIONSHIP

In the next pages we propose two ways to work on establishing effective relationships between board and executive. The first will help you decide the way you wish to divide major leadership tasks. The second deals specifically with some ways to clarify those tasks once decisions about who does what are made.

Create Your Own Way of Working Together

The extra underline here should be on "own." It is your working relationship, your organization; you know best its particular character and more so, what you as responsible leader want for it. Resist advice that begins "boards should always..." or "executives ought never..." There are few "always" and "nevers" in the world of organizational life. There are lots of special cases, special people forging working relationships in ways that work best for them.

You need to decide what will be your predominant way of working together in your organization with your board members and your executive. That should help you be more effective, more often enjoying what you are doing, and feeling mostly in control of where you are and where you are going.

Generally speaking, boards and executives tend to operate in one of four ways. While they are not entirely distinct from one another, for purposes of discussion and decision about how you wish to operate, here they are in brief:

1. Board initiates and decides, executive receives and implements.

This is probably the most formal way of running an organization. The board is strong, well in control and the executive is clear about professional activity based on board directives. This tends to work well where board members are designated representatives from other organizations or control the funding sources. In this model, executives do well who are good at the faithful carrying out of the decisions made by the board.

2. Executive proposes, board disposes.

The executive takes the lead in developing new ideas, programs, and funding. The board critiques, amends, and decides. Board activity is focused on review and response with the executive acting as initiator. At best, a fine balance is reached between executive creativity and board control. At worst, the executive ends up lobbying ideas and the organization moves toward an adversarial mode with innovation and creativity on one side and practicality and control on the other.

3. Executive acts, board is informed and consulted.

Small organizations, or those fashioned around the abilities of a strong leader, often function in this manner. The board acts as consultant as needed and the executive stays in the lead with the ideas and their execution. If the paid leadership is consistent in consulting the board and the board is willing to have a more passive role, this can work well. If the executive fails to consult or makes decisions or takes action which embarrasses the board, it does not work well.

4. Board and executive jointly initiate and implement.

This operates best where boards are willing to share power and executives are willing to share programs. The prudential wisdom is that boards must set policy, not executives; and, executives must design and run programs, not boards. Like all prudential wisdom, this advice is mostly wise and prudent. It does tend to keep board and CEO from being flexible enough to use the rich variety of knowledge and ability that exists in the leadership of an organization.

Most organizations have boards and executives with a mix of creativity and practicality, policy making and program development skills. Effective organizations find ways of using the varieties of abilities without being confined by strict role definitions. This does not work well where the executive or board members, for whatever reason, want well-defined and protected roles.

There are, of course, a near infinite number of ways to run an organization. Your own way may be a mix of the above or something quite different. The four presented are a starting point for discussions about partnership building between the board and executive presently responsible for the life of your organization.

Clarify your roles

In a newly formed partnership everything is subject to change: policies, procedures, programs, and staffing. Moving these changes through an organization in a way that is satisfying for everyone will challenge a new partnership. If done thoughtfully and well, it will set a positive model of process for subsequent organizational change. If done poorly (too much hard selling, absence of good advice and clear consent), the recuperation period will linger and affect months of leadership interaction.

In clarifying leadership responsibility at the beginning of a new partnership, there are three considerations:

1. What are the basic categories within your organization in which change may take place (for example, program, marketing, funding)?

2. Which are the usual steps that occur in making a change (for example, proposing, deciding, implementing)?

3. What leaders take responsibility for each step (for example, board, executive, board committee)?

PRIMARY LEADERSHIP FUNCTIONS WITHIN AN ORGANIZATION

The following matrix will assist you in thinking clearly about how you want your partnership to work. First, use a separate form for each category. Second, check opposite the Leadership Role the primary place where that role would be carried out. In some cases you may decide that a particular function may occur in two or more places. You might want to have board members and the executive fill out the forms separately, then discuss them and work toward a consensus. In either case, try to get in an experimental frame of mind and try out a new way for a year then decide how well it works.

Use one form for each of the following: Mission and Purposes, Program and Services, Marketing and Public Relations, Planning and Evaluation, Funding and Finance, Administration and Staffing.

Responsible Leader(s)

Leadership Function	Executive	Board President	Committee Chair	Board Committee	Full Board
Initiate					
Formulate					
Propose					
Decide					
Implement					
Monitor					
Evaluate					
Reformulate					

Chapter 7

The Primary Partnership: President and Executive

I f things go as they should your becoming president was not without the approval of the executive director. In our view no executive should solely determine who the board president will be. Likewise, no nominating committee will nominate a board president without first consulting the executive. So if being president means your executive feels at least okay about that, you are off to a good start. So now what?

Well, understanding that your relationship with the executive is a major key to the health and effectiveness of your organization, you need to think about it and work on it with no small amount of energy. And, just as there is no one best way to make a marriage, there is no one best way to make a productive president-executive relationship. Here are three that we have seen work well. They are not entirely distinct one from another but in each there is a special emphasis.

THREE KINDS OF PARTNERSHIPS

The conceptual partnership is one in which president and executive tend to be intellectual people full of energy for new and different ideas. It is clear to the rest of the board in meetings and the daily round of activity that each partner is a thinker-planner-debater who thrives on topics related to the conduct of business, the nuances of mission, the societal issues which most impinge upon the organization, and all the various strategies that might be employed to further engage individual board members. This tone will set an organizational style that values and encourages discussion on bigger issues, imagination about overall direction, and attention to the role of the organization in the landscape of not-for-profit organizations in your community.

The companionable partnership is experienced by the rest of the board as a mutually supportive relationship. One board president we know says to the executive, "my job is to make you look good and yours is to make me look good." That attitude of giving away credit, of sharing the power and authority, of looking out for the well being of the other creates a feeling within the board and organization of friendliness, supportiveness, and trust. In this atmosphere the board grows to be low on competition, high on praise and generally a warm and welcoming group of leaders. This particular president-executive partnership, just like the conceptual partnership, may or may not be you. Or you may be attracted to some aspects of each.

The coaching partnership rests on fairly wide differences in leadership experience and sophistication. Sometimes you as president will end up working with a bright new executive who has yet to have the full charge "chief" executive experience. Occasionally those new to the board presidency will work alongside a seasoned executive who has experienced several board presidents. If you are the more seasoned one, having been a board president before, you are potentially in a position to be of help to your colleague who is newer to the task of executive. You will likely participate in that person's growth, while at the same time improving the effectiveness of the organization. It can, of course, be delicate as any mentoring relationship can be, but it can also be very rewarding for both partners. The newer executive can feel supported, nurtured in their professional growth. An experienced president can feel the satisfaction of engaging in the growth of another and seeing the benefits for the whole organization.

So, there are three predominant models. Of course there are more and yes there are an infinite number of combinations. But perhaps these three, read and discussed by you and your executive early in your term of office, might help form how you work together and do so in a way that makes that working together more satisfying for both of you.

As we have implied, the board president-executive relationship deserves special care. While the two of you may be friends, the relationship also needs healthy portions of mutual respect, open communication, and clarity of roles. This can happen more easily if the president is in office for two or three years rather than one. It will also more often happen if you two designate regular times to meet: for board meeting preparation, problem solving and discussions about personnel, and other matters affecting the well being of the organization.

FOUR CRUCIAL CONVERSATIONS

Speaking of conversations, we have had many with the various executives with whom we have worked over the years. Four stand out in our minds as being particularly rewarding. For what it is worth here they are. You may want to give them a try. If so make sure you create some quiet, relaxed time together so that they have the best chance to do well.

About goals

Try a conversation about goals for your term of office. You bring to this role different qualities than the previous board president. We urge you not to shy away from leaving your own special mark, your own unique influence on the organization. That might be a broader funding base, a new and stronger relationship with the media, the extension of a program to a new audience, or something else.

About environment

Try another conversation about the kind of environment the two of you want to create. Maybe it is the permission to ask more questions, to inquire and even challenge reports and proposals. Maybe it is to ensure that more time is spent on big issues and less energy given over to small details. Maybe it is promptness of beginnings and endings of meetings, and maneuvering through an efficient agenda. Whatever the special environmental condition you wish to bring about, merely announcing it won't make it happen. The two of you need to embody it, model it for the rest of the leaders, see that it happens in practice.

About what to avoid

Try a conversation about what you want to avoid — not big obvious things like "misunderstandings," but things like private conversations in board meetings while business is being conducted, surprising the other with a new proposal in a board meeting, too-full agendas, re-discussing and re-deciding an issue, allowing any one or two board members to dominate a discussion, creating structure and practice in which the executive committee becomes the in-group, the quasi-board. You no doubt will have your own favorite list of things you don't want to happen.

About board meetings

Try yet another conversation about all the issues that surround board meetings, the before, during, and after tasks that one or the other of you will inherit. Following is a list of some examples that executives and board presidents divide in different ways:

1. Writing the meeting announcement reminder

2. Telephoning "special" people to get them there

3. Seeing that minutes are ready for presentation

4. Creating the agenda

5. Writing the agenda for distribution

6. Arranging the meeting space

7. Arranging the refreshments, if any

8. Making sure minutes are taken and checked

9. Thanking special guests

10. Inquiring about members not present

These are small items, but they not only contribute to well-run meetings, they can also fall unattended between the two of you if not discussed.

The focus here has been on getting your partnership off to a good start. A "good start" means at least three things: that your partnership is uniquely yours, designed for your special situation; that there is clarity between the two of you about who is responsible for the various organizational functions during your time of office; and that the executive-board president relationship is attended to, respected, and understood to be where the character and tone of the whole organization is shaped.

Part III

Some Unexpected Essentials

Chapter 8

The Year-Round Nominating Committee

A year-round nominating committee effort is crucial for at least two reasons. First, because new faces are good. In too many cities a relatively small number of people serve on boards and mostly, we believe, because the recruitment usually goes something like this, "Well it's November again, do you know anyone who might like to be on our board?" That narrow, last-minute process is sure to produce a board of known neighbors and colleagues who may or may not care about your mission and will pretty much look like every other board in town. Secondly, because people who are crazy about your mission are good. And that takes searching, asking, checking. That takes months, not weeks. But hidden in neighborhoods, work places, and social and service organizations are people who are wild about nutrition or seniors or dance or any number of different missions. They can be found if you give yourself time and if you believe, as we do, that new faces who care greatly about your mission are important because they can challenge and re-enliven trusted board veterans.

This section will not eliminate the possibility of making poor choices of board members. But it will increase the odds that your search for leaders will be an enhancing experience and produce a team of leaders appropriate for your organization. It may be the most important action that president and executive cause to happen. These key partners need to exercise great care in selecting the broader team of leadership partners.

Now, the promised detail. What follows are guidelines, processes, and forms that you can use as you sit with and instruct the nominating committee about its work. For that matter copy this out, read through it together and decide what and how you can make best use of it in your situation.

We assume you have a nominating committee with control over its recommendation. If your constitution provides for the board to elect its own members or for the membership to choose board members, the nominating committee is a major influence. Where board members are elected by the general public or selected by an outside appointing authority, suggestions are in order but influence is limited. In any case, exercise all the influence you can in understanding your board's membership needs and finding the best people to fill those positions. The term "best people" means a lot of things, not the least of which is people whose enthusiasm for your mission matches your own and people with whom you can enjoy the carrying out of that mission.

Make sure you pursue various networks when selecting new members. Current board members commonly go only to their comfortable friendship networks. This is not a bad place to start, but limited if that is where it ends. Many people other than board members have a stake in your organization, including funders, government officials, community leaders, past board members, and past and present clients. Along with their interest comes a perception about the board, its composition, and effectiveness. Ask them about the issues. The impressions of these groups of people are useful. Their sense of the kind of people your board should be recruiting is important. You then may amend your conclusions about new member selection. By soliciting suggestions from these sources, you develop new networks, broaden your perspective, and extend your reach into the community.

Don't underestimate the public relations potential of a well-thought-out and efficiently executed search for board members. Communicating clearly about your organization's mission and board member functions and responsibilities will further your organization's good image wherever you present your case.

Now, forward to three issues that will help you find and engage a leadership team that works well for your organization: Reflecting on Your Present Board Membership, Communicating During Recruitment, and Beginning Well.

REFLECTING ON YOUR PRESENT BOARD MEMBERSHIP

Demographics, skills and community sectors, and motives for membership are three lenses through which to look at your present board. You can consider the first two through sample profiles provided in this section. We also offer a check list of motives for board participation which might be useful. All three will help you know your current board better and therefore what you want to add as you seek new members.

Demographics

A demographic profile of the present board may help you better visualize the mix and balance of membership. In the following form, place the number of board members in each category. The resulting composite will help direct your selection process once your board has decided the right balance and representation for your organization. Having that discussion with present board members will raise important issues and perhaps suggest important changes in the demography of leadership.

Demographics

Criteria	Number of Board Members in Each Category	Criteria	Number of Board Members in Each Category
Age Youth 20-35 35-50 51-65 Over 65		**Residence** Center City 1. 2. Etc. City Neighborhood 1. 2. Etc.	
Sex Male Female		Suburban Area 1. 2. Etc. Rural Area 1. 2. Etc.	
Race/Ethnicity African-American Asian-American Hispanic/Latin-American Native American Caucasian Other			

Board Skills and Community Sectors

Of course in board member selection, you must consider factors other than demography. The matrix on the following page may assist in understanding your present board membership relative to significant leadership criteria. A composite profile will help determine gaps that make a difference. Again, it is up to you to determine that special mix of skills and sector representation that works best for your board.

Board Member Motives

People serve on boards for a mix of reasons. In any given organization, a judgment usually develops about which motives are good, which are better or which are unacceptable. The motives on the following chart are present within most boards. Which are you most looking for? How would your present board rate the acceptability of these motives? With which motives would present board members identify themselves and what does that mean for the selection of new members?

Have present board members check their top two or three reasons for participating. (Probably no one does anything for one pure reason, so allow for flexibility). Talk about the results and what that means for your board. Second, what does that suggest about the kind of people you should recruit for leadership? Finally, reflecting on motives is probably best done with lively good humor versus the intensity of psychoanalysis.

Board Skills and Sectors

Skills	Number of Present Board Members	Community Sectors	Number of Present Board Members
Programming		Business	
Finance		Professional	
Fundraising		Government	
Personnel		Union	
Public Relations		Volunteer	
Legal matters		Clients or customers	
Building & Grounds		Cultural	
Planning		Educational	
Board Development		Etc.	
Etc.			

Motives for Board Participation

Motive	Relative influence High to Low				
Commitment to cause	❏	❏	❏	❏	❏
Affiliation need	❏	❏	❏	❏	❏
Political aspirations	❏	❏	❏	❏	❏
Utilization of talent	❏	❏	❏	❏	❏
Learning & self-improvement	❏	❏	❏	❏	❏
Civic responsibility	❏	❏	❏	❏	❏
Business contacts	❏	❏	❏	❏	❏
Public visibility	❏	❏	❏	❏	❏
Personal/social contacts	❏	❏	❏	❏	❏
Development of hobby or interest	❏	❏	❏	❏	❏
Status	❏	❏	❏	❏	❏
Career enhancement	❏	❏	❏	❏	❏
Other: _____	❏	❏	❏	❏	❏
Other: _____	❏	❏	❏	❏	❏
Other: _____	❏	❏	❏	❏	❏

COMMUNICATING DURING RECRUITMENT

Of course during board member recruitment, you will want to be sending messages about your organization's history, vision, and present challenges. Make sure you receive information as well. Recruitment is less a sales pitch and more the establishment of a relationship with a new neighbor. That means you need to listen for common interests and shared values that match the essence of what your organization is about. The demographics and skills may fit well with your profile, but remember, you are looking for someone who has a special personal connection to the central purpose of your organization.

On the sending messages side, often heard complaints from board members include that no one made clear how much time would be involved or that one responsibility would be to contribute money. Be up front and clear about the twin powerhouses of time and money. Consider these sample issues that you should be prepared to address with potential board members.

About time

How many board meetings do you hold a year? How much time is spent at each? What is the expectation for committee service and attendance at organizational functions? In many organizations the total is equal to 60 to 80 hours or one to two work weeks per year. Must everyone do all the work? What portion is acceptable and in line with the present practice of the board? When recruiting or when telling your story, be sure everyone is telling the same story and the whole story.

About money

Most boards find it useful in fundraising if they can state that all board members contribute financially to the organization. Some set a standard for giving for all and others believe that there are a variety of ways to give, and that money is but one. Professional service time is another. Problems most often occur when board members discover the money rules after getting on the board. Whatever yours are (and they may need discussing), state them in advance. Also clarify expenses connected with attending board meetings and doing board business. Considerations such as travel, per diem, and long distance telephone calls vary from board to board.

Some final questions

All qualities important to board membership cannot be captured in a profile. There are questions worth thinking about and sometimes asking of potential board members. The following have been useful to a variety of boards:

1. How has the person demonstrated a serious interest in our mission?

2. What is the person's potential for board leadership?

3. Is the person available only for consultation?

4. Is the person available for planning and development?

5. Is the person available for committee work?

6. Does the person represent a client group of the organization, and a possible conflict of interest?

7. Can the person be an effective link to important constituent groups?

8. Is this someone you will enjoy working with?

BEGINNING WELL

What happens after a potential board member says "OK, consider me interested"? Probably, they do not become official board members until a vote by the full board. That should be made clear to the candidate during recruiting. Most nominating committees will report the date and time of the first meeting. Sometimes the board chair will write a letter of welcome. Two important matters remain: how are the new members oriented and how is it decided which committee responsibility, if any, they will have?

Some boards have board member orientation conducted by a personnel or board development committee. Other boards appoint a seasoned board member to a one-on-one mentoring role. Sometimes the executive director has a partial responsibility to orient new members to the board. You need to decide what works best for your situation. Matching new board members with appropriate committees should be done with some balance between the board's needs and the special interests and abilities of the new recruit. All certified public accountants should not be on the finance committee and all marketing professionals will not want to end up on the public relations committee. Boards, like other work groups, tend to function best when most of the people most of the time are doing what they like best. The right decisions here will assist greatly in successfully integrating them into the life of the board. Consider the following:

Things to listen for: Learning something new from a recruit

- What is the new member's view, as a relative outsider, of your organization's special niche in the community?

- What does the new member perceive to be the unique character/culture of the organization that needs to be preserved and nourished?

- What does he know your organization for doing well that needs to continue?

- What aspects of your organization seem to her to be less well developed and in need of strengthening?

- What confuses or weakens your image in the community?

- For what in the organization does the new recruit want to take some responsibility?

Things to say: Only the crucial and that, succinctly

- What the initial need, spark, or enthusiasm was that got your organization going.

- How that initial focus has developed and changed.

- What the three or four most important challenges are in the next 12 to 24 months.

- What you worry most about.

- In what areas the organization needs help or new leadership.

- Information concerning finance, other board and committee members, contributors, meeting times and dates, by-laws, and reporting requirements, in addition to other basic organizational information.

With any luck that amount of detail will take you through a thoughtful process of board member nominations from assessment of your present board to preparation of new members. Getting the right mix of people in place for the future leadership of your board may be one of the most significant things you do.

Chapter 9

Hearing Things: The Many Voices of the Board

Part III:
Some Unexpected Essentials

Once upon a while... yes, here comes an illustrative story... there was a board president named Helen Boyse. She loved old houses, antiques, city neighborhoods, and lace curtains. She had generally figured out how to fill her life with and enjoy all these things and wished the same for others. That is how she became involved on the board of Preservation Central, a historic district on the upper east side of a Midwestern city of half a million people. How she became president was this rare combination of loving something very much (in this case historic preservation), being able to speak about it in a clear and compelling way, and being the kind of open, honest and dependable person that people like being around.

She discovered something very important in the first of her three years as president. The board members (all seventeen of them) seemed to have opinions that ranged from strong to emphatic. Furthermore, since that board met every other month there was lots of time to store up opinions between meetings. At the meetings it was hard to stay on any one subject because these various stored up opinions kept popping up and seldom in the right places. At first Helen thought of this as an unfortunate thing. So many talented and outspoken people gathered in one place going off into several often unrelated places. She sometimes fell into longing for the shy, "Whatever you think's best" people she knew from volunteering on a committee at the local chamber of commerce.

But she came up with an idea that changed everything (well not everything). During the year she would schedule a private breakfast or lunch with every board member. It would be a "tell me what is on your mind about our organization" meeting. She would ask them to describe their own involvements and satisfactions over the years and describe, as well, any frustration they had working with Preservation Central. She would try to understand what their hopes were for the organization, what programs, old or new, they most cared about and even get their opinions about how the organization might better structure or run itself. And perhaps most important, she got to know their special gifts and just how those might connect with Preservation Central so that everybody would win. Now these were one and one half hour meetings and there were sixteen which means a hefty twenty-four hour commitment.

But Helen heard a lot of things — several for the first time — and she grew to appreciate even more the many (and strong) voices of this board. And another thing happened. The board meetings got better (funny thing). Maybe that was the most important discovery and the best thing about all these breakfasts and lunches — board members' thoughts were eagerly considered so they no longer had to work so hard at board meetings to be heard.

Whatever you conclude, we conclude that we prefer board members who care deeply and express strongly. While they can be hard work we prefer that to trying to motivate people to speak up. We conclude that getting to know board members one-on-one and being able to listen to what their issues are is well worth the time. We conclude that the board president's job of talent scout — of understanding what board members are good at and enjoy and connecting that with the life of the organization — just may be some of the most important work that we do.

That's the transition sentence needed to move us to structuring the board and its meetings so that board members are not only well-heard but meaningfully involved. This one we are going to get at through descriptions of how two different boards that we know well structure the work and time of their boards to see that all board members are feeling involved and useful. (By the way, involved and useful are two very key things. You'll have a happier more productive board if you can figure out how to get both done.) Examples follow that may help.

STRUCTURING THE WORK AND TIME OF YOUR BOARD

For ease of comparison we selected two boards of about the same size — 15 and 17 members — with budgets in the $500,000 to $600,000 range, and both roughly in the business of providing human services. We do believe that regardless of your mission, one of these two models, or a combination of them, will work just fine.

Advance Unlimited

Advance Unlimited is an organization that supports teenage youth who are unlikely to go on to higher education due to financial and/or family difficulties, but who may be more likely to succeed given timely advice and financial support. The chart, which follows on the next page, outlines how they have structured their work.

Group Meetings	Board Officer	Staff Involved	Number of Meetings
Board	President	Executive	10 yearly
Exec. Committee	President	Executive	6 yearly
Program	Vice President	Program Director	10 yearly
Finance	Treasurer	Financial Officer	10 yearly
Financial Devel.	President	Devel. Director	6 yearly
Facilities	Board member	Admin. Asst.	4 yearly
Planning & Eval.	Vice President	Executive	6 yearly
Personnel	Board member	n/a	3 yearly
Marketing & PR	Secretary	Part-time Market. Director	6 yearly

Of course, some things are not easily accommodated by the above chart. The executive committee is comprised of the four officers (President, Vice President, Secretary and Treasurer) plus the board chairs of each of the committees. The executive committee is careful not to do business which is then repeated at the board meeting. Its function is to review the progress of the committees and in so doing, develop a plan for the board meeting.

Note that the board president is fairly intimately involved in three areas: the board, the executive committee and the committee on fund development. Note also that staff people meet with committees that are related to the work which they do. Only the executive attends the meetings of the board and executive committee. While this model is fairly standard it is also very workable.

Now you can use the blank chart on the next page (copy it out) to have a discussion about how your board currently functions and about how you all would like to change.

Group Meetings	Board Officer	Staff Involved	Number of Meetings

Transitions

Transitions does its work primarily with women who are in the process of making educational and career decisions. Like Advance Unlimited, they have been in existence for over twenty years and are in a reasonably good financial situation. The chart which follows outlines a different way of structuring work.

Group Meetings	Board Officer	Staff Involved	Number of Meetings
Board	President	Executive	4 yearly
Exec. Committee	President	Executive	3 yearly
Ed. Programs	Board Member	Direct. of Ed.	6 yearly
Counseling Pgms.	Board Member	Direct. of Couns.	6 yearly
Finance & Fund.	Treasurer	Financial Officer	6 yearly
Board Devel.	Vice President	n/a	6 yearly
Human Resources	Board Member	Executive	6 yearly
Outreach & PR	Board Member	Asst. Director	6 yearly

This is not better or worse, only different. There are far fewer board and executive meetings, which forces the work more into committees. The important function of planning and evaluation is no longer in a specific committee but carried out by the Executive Committee. There are two major aspects of programming, each assigned to a separate committee. There is a new committee, Board Development, charged with enhancing the abilities of board members. Each board meeting contains a twenty-minute board development presentation. There is a Human Resources committee which is charged with the traditional personnel functions, as well as staff development and the recruitment and training of volunteers.

You might choose to copy Transitions' chart and use it as the basis for a discussion on aspects of the model that might be incorporated into your organization's current way of working.

REVIEWING YOUR BOARD'S INVOLVEMENT IN ORGANIZATIONAL TASKS

One more chart which might be the basis for good discussion on your board focuses not on the details of what committees and how often they meet but on eight essential board tasks that are fairly unavoidable. It gives you the opportunity to think through these tasks and which individuals or committees might share in them.

You may want to begin by rating things the way they are and then redo the form according to the ideal for your organization. It is likely that neither the board nor the executive always formulates or always implements. What you are looking for is the predominant pattern, the way it most often works. And, equally important, you are looking for the way you want it to be in the future.

We believe it preferable to discuss your observations with the executive in preparation for a lively conversation with your full board. Remember that all of this is about creating structures and patterns for working that maximally engage board members and are more likely to get the work of your organization done in an effective and efficient manner.

Who Does What

Organizational Function	Board President	Board	Executive Committee	Specific Committee	Executive
Create/initiate					
Formulate/ conceptualize					
Propose/present					
Decide/approve					
Implement/ execute					
Monitor/ manage					
Assess/ evaluate					
Reformulate/ refine					

ENGAGING EX-BOARD MEMBERS

If you have done your listening well and if you have structured the board so that all members have a good and useful place to participate, people will like being on your board and have separation anxiety when they go off for a mandatory year's "sabbatical" or perhaps not to return. After such thoughtful cultivation, it would be wasteful for the organization to lose them and sad for them to be separated from a role that meant a lot to them.

So how about this idea we've heard about: a board alumni group with a clever name like "Board Infinitum," "Above Board," or "Over Board"? The key to success in the situation we know about is that the group meets seldom — two times a year. The other thing is they have NO real work to do, especially not fundraising. This particular group has lunch with the executive and board president every six months (in fact the 15 or so are treated to lunch). They get to hear all the latest about what has happened and what is planned. From time to time they are asked to consult on a specific issue (what might we do to get better media coverage), or assist in finding a particular volunteer (who could help us think about developing a web site). Mostly it is social and it keeps a sense of organizational community going. It is a way of continuing to acknowledge the importance of people who care a lot and have given much. It helps people feel okay about leaving the board and it helps the organization stay in significant touch with people whose continued good feelings about the organization can help in so many direct and indirect ways.

Chapter 10

Choreographing the Board Meeting

W e know you have a picture of what it takes to do a special event, beginning with plans and invitations through to clean-up and thank you. You'll no doubt remember having to think about the messages you want to convey, structuring the time so that the movement from one thing to the next seems effortless, tending to all the details of space, and determining what people sip and where they sit. With the complexities of special event planning and orchestration in mind, we'd like you to begin thinking about your board meetings as such special events requiring a similar level of thorough planning, thoughtful consideration of the order of things, and careful attention to detail. That is why we chose the word choreograph — not a simple matter when it comes to a dance company. Or if you prefer, orchestrate, an equally complex matter when it comes to a symphony.

What we most wish to convey is that you have very few hours in a year when you have the leadership of your organization together in one place. This gathering of the leadership to exercise tender loving care over the life of your organization is in fact a very special event that deserves your very best. That is why we plan on spending a little time (a few pages) with you to help you think about it. We are aware that this may be one of the most important places for you to do your reading and thinking in tandem with your executive. The executive after all will be at the board meeting and what each of you does or doesn't do, how the two of you interact and assist one another will set the tone of the meeting and largely determine its success. So, we offer two aspects for your consideration here and for future discussion with your executive: one is agenda creation (choreographing, orchestrating) and the other the actual meeting (with some hints about being there together in one place).

CREATING THE AGENDA

One board president we know meets with the executive two weeks before the board meeting to review how the previous meeting went and to form the agenda for the next. The advantage of two weeks is that it is close enough that most of the issues will be apparent by then and far enough in advance that there is still time to send out the completed agenda. They have also over the months begun to agree on a few general notions about the agenda. One notion, with which we also agree, is that if every meeting has at least one hefty issue that requires the board to use its imagination and exercise its discussion skills, there is a far better chance that members will come away feeling the meeting was, in fact, significant. Too often agendas are too long and full of minor issues and matters of strategy and logistics. Boards need the experience of being led to the bigger, overarching issues that command their intellects and their creative energies. One arts organization opened its meeting with the topic "What do you believe to be the brow level of our performances: too high, too low? Which way should we move?" A child-serving agency asked its board to grapple with the issues of the danger of dependency on a single funding source. The local international center board discussed the history and changes in immigration policies in our country over the past two decades and the effect on its local programming. These are the kinds of lofty topics that elevate and enhance the thinking of your board.

And actually, it's not a bad idea to start your meeting there. Meetings have a way of finding a level of significance early on. So if you begin with the small stuff you are more likely to have a small-stuff kind of meeting. Whereas beginning with the big issues sets a tone of importance and depth that will, with any luck, permeate the whole meeting.

Ending well is also a good thing. We know of one small college board that always ends with "good news from around the campus." We find this to be a nice and memorable way to end a meeting — hearing five or six things to make you proud of your organization. We know of another board of a drug treatment agency that ends with personal letters from clients, news clippings, and announcements about recognitions and awards received by board and staff members. This is also good stuff to have in mind as you depart the board meeting. Starting with significance, ending well — with first and third acts like that, the play has got to be good.

Sometimes we have heard board members complain that they are never quite sure what is expected of them on a specific agenda item. It usually goes something like this, "So do you want to hear what I think, want me to just nod my head yes or no, or just let you know I heard what was reported?" A board of a children's museum handles it this way. They organize the agenda into three broad categories: items for discussion and decision, items for ratification, and items for information. Actually they put them in that order which ensures that the bigger issues are addressed first. Then it is always clear what is being asked: i.e. we want you to discuss and decide about our new admissions rates, we want you to listen and approve (or disapprove) the report of the finance committee on spending $5,000 for a new auditor, we want you to know that during the past month we were able to replace our marketing director. Try organizing the agenda items so it is clear what is expected of your board members.

Keeping in touch

Another one you might want to consider comes to us from a chamber of commerce executive in a town of 150,000. She talks about and writes about how important it is for board members to "keep in touch." But keeping in touch for her involves far more than mere "What's been going on in your life." Here's the way she expresses it.

"Our board members know the value and necessity of keeping in close touch with each other. These additional special touches keep board meetings spirited and inspired. Not all can happen at every board meeting but one or two at each likely will change the character of your gatherings.

1. Touch on History: Keep board members in touch with what has gone on before them. A history or time-line developed at a board retreat could be permanently displayed and reviewed occasionally. Knowing the organization's history helps explain "how we got to where we are, why we do things the way we do, and who made things happen."

2. Touch the Mission: Keep the organization's mission statement visible to the board by printing it on the back of their name placards (tents) which are used at every board meeting. Each year the board could revisit the mission statement to rephrase it in their own words, in their unique way, thereby, keeping it fresh and easily understood.

3. Touch the Public: Keep the group centered on those they serve by hearing a beneficiary report or by visiting the served group or agency or through video presentations of those served. Allow board members some time to brainstorm who "customers" are to increase awareness of the organization's wide impact on the community.

4. Touch the Future: Help keep board members focused in the right direction by looking at your organization's vision periodically or creating a vision together. Make dreams real by breaking them into achievable pieces, and allow board members to choose the pieces to which they will commit.

5. Keep in Touch: Remember absentee board members. Use phone calls, reminders, special notes. Making personal contact is the way to include all and let them know you care about them. All organizations are really in the people business — they exist of people, by people, and for people. It is important to really like and care for people in order to work with and serve them well."

Sharing responsibility for agenda items

One final matter you may wish to clarify before the board members are in the room. Each board president-executive partnership develops its own way of making the board meetings work well. While there are some general guidelines, the specifics can be decided in a way that works for the two of you.

Though the traditional expectation is that the president formally conducts the meeting by proceeding through the agenda, in some not-for-profit organizations the board president simply opens or closes the meeting and takes votes on issues with the rest of the meeting run by the executive director.

There are some things each will always do. Identify those. For example, your partnership might decide that the president always will present, modify and proceed through the agenda and the executive director always will be responsible for the staff report (written or verbal).

Other items could vary. You could decide that, at budget time, it is more appropriate for the executive director to explain the proposed budget. But if the budget contains new salary increases, for instance, the board president may choose to present that information. If the organization has a finance director, then the presentation obviously could be delegated to that person.

There are some matters for which both of you probably will want to assume joint (or equal) responsibility. Ensuring that the board meeting begins and ends on time is one of our favorite examples.

The key is that, acting in partnership, you identify aspects of the board meeting for which each is best suited. We hope that both of you will consider the benefits of a shared, team approach to leading meetings and, through thoughtful planning, will balance your leadership styles, gifts and actions to achieve efficiency and harmony. When the leadership partners skillfully balance the act of leading, a level of professional elegance is achieved that will be appreciated by the board members.

You may wish to make use of the following checklist to determine your own special design for the leadership of the board meeting.

The Balancing Act of Leading Board Meetings

You decide who...	Board President	Executive Director	Both Share
Begins and ends board meeting on time.	❏	❏	❏
Welcomes group; makes everyone feel at ease.	❏	❏	❏
Guides last-minute changes.	❏	❏	❏
Draws out knowledge and resources of board members.	❏	❏	❏
Gives staff reports and updated information.	❏	❏	❏
Proceeds through agenda.	❏	❏	❏
Modifies agenda.	❏	❏	❏
Restates each item and brings to closure.	❏	❏	❏
Summarizes progress.	❏	❏	❏
Assigns action items to appropriate people.	❏	❏	❏
Encourages interaction; draws out quiet people. ❏	❏	❏	❏
Applauds volunteer efforts, thanks group, celebrates achievements. ❏	❏	❏	❏
Add your own:	❏	❏	❏
_____	❏	❏	❏
_____	❏	❏	❏
_____	❏	❏	❏

THE MEETING IN PROGRESS

Robert(a)'s Rules (of Order) in short

You probably cannot avoid a once-in-a-while bow in the direction of Robert's Rules of Order. They are far too formal for many situations and far too detailed for many more. But occasionally they can prove useful. So in case you are not quite familiar, here is a greatly condensed version done well we think by Brian O'Connell, for years the executive director of The Independent Sector. In his *The Board Member's Book*, this appears in a chapter aptly titled "Robert's Rules of Order — Demystified".

Starting at the most elementary level, this is the way a group formally makes a decision:

> • One of the members will move that a decision be made (this is proposing that the board go on record in favor of a certain definite action).

> • Another member of the group will second the motion, which means "support" for the action proposed. (The second is necessary to be certain that the issue is of interest to more than one person.)

> • Once the motion has been made and seconded, there is discussion, clarification, and debate.

> • When the subject has been covered fully, there is the vote.

> • Prior to both discussion and vote, the person in the chair should restate the motion to be certain everyone knows what is being discussed and decided.

That should suffice for ninety-six percent of the business in most organizations. However, if you are a quasi-public institution or dealing with highly controversial issues with community-wide ramifications, a stricter use of Robert's Rules may become essential.

An effective meeting checklist

Having struggled through (sometimes sailed through) more than a few (hundred) board meetings ourselves, here is a list of our own favorite things worth noting (the first is not more important than the last, it's just that we thought of them in this order):

1. Being polite is a good thing at dinner but at board meetings, if it means no disagreements allowed, it's not such a good thing.

2. Too much information on too many pages is confusing and can inhibit good, clear discussions.

3. Too little information will cause any thoughtful board member to put off a decision until all the necessary information is available.

4. Demonstrating that you are able to reach healthy consensus out of initial disagreement encourages board members to express divergent opinions.

5. See that everyone has the opportunity to express themselves by moderating those who tend to be dominant and assisting those who tend to be shy.

6. Decisions reached after some difficulty should be acted upon promptly so that it is worth it all.

7. Don't go back over and open up decisions reached after long and thoughtful discussions unless significant new circumstances have arisen.

8. Respect everyone's time. Starting promptly discourages tardiness. Ending promptly encourages focused discussions (and will make you popular).

9. Have a clear and fast decision process and insist that everyone respects it and does not go around it.

10. Finally, practice some medium-to-small issues in the following categories with the board so that when the big ones come along you will be experienced at dealing with them.

- Practice making changes in program and in administration
- Practice reviewing and assessing things
- Practice facing the controversial

Chapter 11

Discovering Your Leadership Voice

"I'm just managing." A curious phrase in human interchange usually uttered in response to "How are you doing today?" "Just managing" means getting by, going through the motions, taking things as they come. That kind of managing is not what you want to be doing as board president. Being a manager, making sure things are done correctly and on time is not a big enough role for you as president. Someone does need to do that. There is, after all, nothing intrinsically wrong with managers. Every organization needs them. But it is possible that our chief problems in the life of organizations today are not because we do not have managers, rather that we do not have leaders. We ask you to consider being a leader. Actually, we ask you to decide, to choose to be a leader by making your own distinctive mark on the life and mission of your organization.

Warren Bennis lists the distinctions between leaders and managers this way:

- The manager administers; the leader innovates

- The manager maintains; the leader develops

- The manager has a short-range view; the leader has a long-range perspective.

- The manager asks how and when; the leader asks what and why

- The manager is a copy; the leader is an original

Original is good and original you are. You may not be Susan B. Anthony giving a lifetime to the right of women to vote. You may not be Winston Churchill calling for great courage in dark times. You may not be Martin Luther King, Jr. powerfully claiming that we could do far better as a nation. But you like they have a distinctive self, a special voice and therefore a unique way of expressing leadership. And it is not that they had perfect models for who to be and what to do as leaders. Their way of leading had integrity, that is their speaking and their acting as leaders followed naturally out of who they were as people. They found their voices, their way, their distinctive leadership expression had great power to do good things.

We urge upon you a sense of your own ability to do good and necessary things while you are board president. Of course pay attention to income, expenses, structures, processes and order, not disregarding the special challenges your organization may be facing during your tenure. But do more and do it in a way that is you.

What might that be? Before giving you some examples of presidents acting on their own special voice, try trekking through these questions:

• What is it about this organization that first drew me to it?

• What is there about me that relates most strongly to the mission of this place?

• What is there that I care most deeply about that can be connected most usefully to what this organization now needs?

• For what aspects of the life of this organization do I wish to take responsibility?

• As board president, what worthy mark do I wish to leave on this place? For what do I wish to be remembered?

These questions may move you closer to discovery of your distinctive voice as a leader. Now three examples that may help you as well. Each is a brief account of how a particular board president expressed his or her particular "thing" in a way that made a significant positive impact on their organizations.

Yolanda was an artist with great sense of color, spirit, and beauty that infected her whole life. She also loved children and cared deeply about their well-being which is why she agreed to be on the board of the Central City Day Care, and largely why she soon emerged as a natural leader and was elected president. Not surprisingly, money and particularly salaries were always a problem, and during her two-year term of office she dedicated herself to addressing that issue in a variety of ways. In fact, after two years their day care teachers and assistants were the best paid in town and all that on a balanced budget. For that she would always be remembered and appreciated, especially by the staff. But the big thing she did that grew directly out of who she was and what she cared about was to change the aesthetic environment of the whole building.

It was drab with too few windows and too much off-white to gray walls. The classrooms were colorful enough with children's art and bright books and toys but the lobby offices and halls were like February. Now if a president with artistic spirit did not make a difference here, who would? She mobilized parents to paint and art collectors and artists to loan bright landscapes and colorful still lifes. There was an instant gallery. The whole environment of the organization changed from February to May and a very powerful and lasting imprint had been made by a board president. She did a very simple thing. She led in a way natural for her and in a direction that matched an organizational need. Yet she did not forget about doing business at the same time.

Ralph, a Human Resource manager in a medium size company, was full of a good, kind-hearted spirit that made people want to be around him. He first got on the board of the leukemia foundation because one of his favorite nieces had been diagnosed with that dreaded disease when she was nine. He felt helpless to do much for her but thought this was one thing he could do for the cause. On the board he helped with special events rather than work on personnel issues as he did daily during the rest of the week. He really didn't think of himself as a leader, but he was so well liked and trusted that after four years he was asked and he accepted the presidency.

While assisting with special events, he realized that too many people in his community didn't know about leukemia and very few realized there was a local foundation. Ralph knew instinctively that part of being a good president was taking care of the basics like (in this case) public relations. He didn't know much about it but did organize a board committee that included outside professionals to address the issues of the relative invisibility of their organization. Things got much better and everyone appreciated this new initiative. He was tending to business.

But the real thing that changed in the life of that organization during the time Ralph was president was the creation of a close community, almost a family-like following. Ralph spent significant time with each board member and the five staff people as well. He listened, he expressed understanding, and he exhibited a regard and kindness for those people that changed the culture of the place. He began each board meeting with personal stories about what had been happening in the lives of board members. Birthday cards magically appeared and announcements were made about special awards and promotions. That was Ralph in action. This was a warm and generous human being practicing the presidency in a way that reflected his warmth and generosity. That organization will never be the same because of that president's willingness to exercise his own distinctive gifts in that setting, all the while taking care of the public relations requirements of the agency.

Donita was a sales representative for a large office supply company. She had spent her early childhood with her family in a poor section of San Juan before coming to this country when she was fourteen. She was active in the Hispanic Community Center, had felt the negative power of discrimination and was not satisfied to be passive about it. She was invited to be on the board of the Ozark Chamber Orchestra because her boss knew the general manager, she loved music and (she suspected) because she was Hispanic. This board service wasn't easy. It was not a particularly friendly place although at least the topic of diversity and inclusivity came up fairly regularly at board meetings. She decided to work on the Facilities Committee because that's what she knew from her day job. After three years Donita chaired the Facilities Committee, after five became Vice President and then in her seventh year (there seemed to be no board terms) agreed to be President.

Knowing the intricacies of inventory management, she recognized that the orchestra's music library was disorganized, with many missing parts and little possibility of finding out what was lacking. With the Artistic Director she completely revamped the system, making it more usable than it had ever been. Donita also took the issue of diversity head on and comprehensively. There was one Asian musician, no people of color on the staff, two minorities out of twenty board members and an audience that was largely suburban middle class whites.

All that changed during her three years as president. How she did it is a compelling story but here not the point. That she did it and that it grew out of her own life experience and conviction is the point. The complexion of audience, staff, and board all changed and that change resulted from a distinctive presidential personality who chose to lead out of who she was on an issue the organization had only talked about.

There are the examples. Board presidents being presidential in ways that are natural to them. Board presidents leading, not merely managing. We hope for you some of the same excitement and satisfaction wherever you practice board leadership.

Chapter 12

An Ethic of Authenticity

W hat we mean by such a lofty phrase as "an ethic of authenticity" is simply how what you value and care about as an organization is carried into action. This is what makes your organization believable or not, trusted or not, well respected or not. This is a crucial one for you to keep your eye on, and we suggest a few ways to help you do just that.

For much of what follows, we can thank seven not-for-profit executives (yes executives, not presidents) who grappled with the issue of ethics in not-for-profit organizations over a two-day retreat. Following the retreat, one of the executives, our Indiana colleague Eric Rogers, captured it as follows:

So what is organizational authenticity? Simply, it is being what you say you are. Simple, but not so simply done. For while it is a relatively straightforward, even exciting task to conceive a vision, it is a more challenging matter to live that vision.

Lack of organizational authenticity may be gauged by measuring the gap between the mission statement and how an organization actually operates. Sensing where there is a difference between words and action and bringing these matters to the attention of the board and the executive may be another one of your most important responsibilities as the president. Indeed, organizational authenticity and leadership may be viewed as bonded as stone and mortar, the foundation upon which every other aspect of the organization will be laid.

Authenticity breeds trust and trust is a source of great power. Yet, it is a power that can be instantly lost by subsequent counterfeit behavior. Indeed, as most of us painfully discover at some time in our lives, trust lost is very difficult to restore. Thus, the degree to which your board can cultivate and preserve organizational authenticity will define the potential for their success as leaders.

Unfortunately, the accelerated pace of organizational life tends to discourage reflection of any kind. Thinking about sometimes obscure and complex ethical considerations usually ends up way down on the list of things to do. What too often results because of the necessary attention to matters urgent and pressing is a numbness to matters ethical. Organizations find themselves blindsided by ethical problems that in the abstract seem obvious but in the practical push of daily activity are overlooked. What follows is a list of often-encountered issues, possibly to serve as a forewarning. These issues appear just about everywhere and no doubt will end up in your very own organizational lap. Consider them now so that you can minimize surprises and decide in advance policy positions on what, for most, are common ethical issues.

Review the issues and examples of each. It is probably worthy of a full board review. Some of the items may seem obvious and self-evident; others are likely to cause discussion. There may be two or three worth addressing in a way that will result in a policy statement for your board. In the course of it all, you may stumble onto an additional two or three that are particularly critical in your organizational situation. Our intent is not that you develop a comprehensive code of ethics but that you become more aware of the ethical issues most likely to impose themselves in your organization and prepare in advance to address what otherwise will be surprising impositions.

A CHECKLIST OF ETHICAL ISSUES

1. Fidelity to Mission
What are the decisions and/or actions most likely to pull the organization in a direction counter to its mission?

Examples: Accepting funds with restrictive purposes or expectations

Attempting to be all things to all people

Bowing to political interests of board members and employees that are beyond the mission of the organization

2. Respect for Individuals
What are the desired standards for the not-for-profit's treatment of board members, staff and constituents?

Examples: Defining compensation levels appropriate to the nature of the organization

Developing employee policies and practices that are reflective of or in harmony with the mission

Setting traditions for the way in which volunteers are selected, managed and recognized

3. Inclusion and Exclusivity

When is it appropriate in the organization for a person or group to make significant unilateral decisions affecting others?

Examples: Determining who should be sought out for advice and consultation on significant decisions

Deciding if some decisions require more than a majority vote

Considering if the board is reflective of the constituency

Considering the influence of committees and organizational structure

Considering who may attend specific committee meetings

4. Openness and Secrecy

What, if anything, should be kept secret or in confidence, and from whom and why?

Examples: Financial information and level of detail

Personnel data and files

Donor information

Proceedings of specific committees

Real estate transactions

Contract information and bidding

5. Conflict of Interest

Are there ways in which we function that result in inappropriate benefit to board members, staff, or constituents?

Examples: Undue constituent influence

Undue financial benefit of board members

Unfair contracting practices involving directors or friends

Personal or intimate relationships within the organization

6. Stewardship and Finance

What should the not-for-profit do to assure that expenditures and resources reflect the present mission and the long-term health of the organization?

Examples: Resource allocation (how available funds are to be expended)

Investment of funds/resources in ways inappropriate to the mission

Spending for the present without regard for meeting the mission in years to come

7. Personal Integrity

What are the personal standards the organization wishes to encourage with respect to honesty and respect for people and property?

Examples: Keeping confidential information confidential (donor records, client data, personnel files)

Honoring commitments (signed and unsigned)

Considering whether the not-for-profit's board and employees are trusted to tell the truth

Establishing integrity with finances as a priority

Presenting financial reports to the public in a straightforward manner

8. Political Integrity

What are the guidelines the organization wishes to use for participation in advocacy, fundraising, and interaction with other organizations?

Examples: Determining how information/data for advocacy purposes will be interpreted

Setting a policy or tradition that discourages undue pressure being placed on prospects for contributions or grants

Deciding what, if any, quid pro quo arrangements shall be encouraged

Setting expectations which discourage the manipulation of volunteers to gain desired results

The above list represents only a number of potential areas for concern. While you may identify other potential ethical issues for your organization, these should demonstrate the general range of issues and the challenge of maintaining authentic behavior.

YOUR RESPONSE
TO THE CHECKLIST

Rare is the organization that needs to deal with all of the above issues. You can play an important role in developing a list of ethical concerns that you believe relate to your own organization.

Once an initial list has been created, the board can discuss which issues are relevant and, of course, consider additional issues. The important part for the president is to initiate a discussion by the board. Once the critical issues have been established, the board can develop appropriate policy responses for each one that is a concern.

Reviewing organizational behavior with an eye to the ethical consequences of the stated mission can be an invigorating experience for the board. This approach can be taken with budgeting, programming, personnel policy, and numerous other aspects of the organization's life. Thus, a simple proposal can take on a new dimension when examined for its impact on and faithfulness to the organization's mission.

For example, experienced presidents have often observed the havoc caused by undue constituent influence or an exclusive approach to solving community challenges. While it may not be the intent, groups often hear only the viewpoints of those in their inner circle. For this reason, these groups become weakened in their ability to incorporate new ideas, deal with change, and reflect all relevant viewpoints.

Money and power can interfere with a not-for-profit's mission and vision. Major donors, due to the size of their contributions and their ties to an organization's board, may try to exercise undue influence. Indeed, they can become the tail wagging the dog. An observed policy on conflict of interest or exclusive behavior can significantly enhance the leader's ability to deal with such challenging situations. The president plays a vital role in assuring the vibrancy of any such policy by reminding the board of its own decisions and enforcing the policies as needed.

Ethical challenges are not always readily apparent and often come about when least expected. The president best serves by keeping the organization in touch with its mission and vigilant for ethical problems that could deter or derail adherence to that mission.

Chapter 13

Presidential Vigilance

Curious title you think. We aren't about to ask you to be the ever-awake and suspicious militant you might picture with the word vigilante. What we have in mind is urging you to be watchful, to take great care in watching over four crucial matters in the life of your organization. You are the one with the best seat from which to see. You should have a clear view of everything. What follows are the five things we'd like you to stare at and watch carefully: the essence, the culture, the life cycle, and the community. Here's looking with you.

WATCHING OVER THE ESSENCE

This is revisiting what makes you distinctive, what is that organizational essence at the heart and soul of who you are and what you do. It will urge you to think more broadly than objectives, more generally yet than goals, and it is less tidy than most mission statements. This discussion should put you back in touch with the initial energy and driving purpose which created your organization. It should also link you to present enthusiasms and future visions.

The following questions are few in number, but they provide a good place for the thoughtful reflection that's so hard to come by in the usual flurry of organizational life.

- What was the special dream that launched our organization?

- How have we amended and enlarged that dream for this present situation?

- How can we now imagine refocusing the resources of this organization?

- What are we best at doing? What is our distinctive competence?

- For what are we valued in the community by its people and institutions?

- What is missing or goes poorly in our community if we are not doing well?

- What do we find ourselves bragging about when we speak to friends about this organization?

- About what do we find ourselves getting most enthusiastic about?

Having thought through these questions, share them with your board. They might very well form the basis for that significant initial agenda item at one of your meetings.

WATCH OVER YOUR CULTURE

This is not culture as in arts and culture. This is the style, tone and feel of your organization. In a way culture is to an organization what personality is to an individual. It is distinctive and you know it when you see it. Culture is a lot of things that go together to make up the character of your organization. The items that follow will not be equal in importance to you. Some will produce a more useful discussion of your special culture. Work with those and skip the others. But do make sure you share at least some of this with your board. Another significant first item on your agenda.

1. Usually, some other organizations do at least some of the things that you do. Exactly where do you fit in the scheme of similar organizations?

2. How are important decisions made in your organization? Is that how you would like it to be in the future?

3. Reflect on the perspective and power of time in your organization.

- How would you characterize your pace and style regarding deadlines, appointments, meeting beginnings and endings?

- What about the overall tone: is it deliberate, hurried, ponderous?

- What is your style of record keeping: is it formal, informal, detailed?

4. What is the importance of space in your organization? Are there important issues about the size and location of offices? Is private space or territoriality a crucial concern?

5. What are your predominant beliefs about human nature?

- People basically look out for themselves first.

- People tend to be hard working and committed.

- People are a mixture of things and are variable.

6. What are your beliefs about people and change?

- People are able to change.

- People are fixed in their behaviors.

- Some people can change, some cannot.

7. Some organizations proceed as though nothing is impossible and any problem can be solved. Some are tentative, less sure about solving problems. Where do you fall along the spectrum?

8. From your experience, what is it that most likely will keep your organization from doing what it wants to do?

9. Organizations operate differently. Here are some predominant modes. How do you see yourselves and where would you like to be?

- It's the way we've always done it.

- This is the right way to do it.

- Let's refer this to a committee and do what they recommend.

- Let's thrash it out in committee and forward it to the board for a decision.

- Let's experiment, see if it works.

- We need some research before we can decide what to do.

As we said, certain ones of these questions may be more interesting and productive than others. Make the list work for you and let your board work on them as well.

WATCH THE LIFE CYCLE

Organizations, like people, have stages in their lives. They are not entirely clear cut nor exactly the same from organization to organization, or person to person. But it is useful for you to understand where your organization is in its life cycle. That knowledge will help you know where you ought to be paying attention and what you ought to be doing, either to enrich the current stage or assist with a move to the next.

The calendar will tell you how old your organization is. It will not tell you which stage it is in. "Life cycle" implies an ongoing variety of organizational transitions. The state you are moving toward requires special leader skills and sensitivities that differ from the stage you are departing.

There are a variety of ways of categorizing organizational life stages. The one outlined here lists five stages to assist you in assessing where you are, where you are likely to go, and what you, as a board president, need to be thinking about and doing.

Organizational Stage	Leader Tasks and Traits
1. The initial dream	High creativity and commitment, flexibility and informal systems; the broad range of abilities of a generalist are needed.
2. Direction/consolidation	Organizational efficiency becomes primary; develop systems, policies, job descriptions. Consolidate and formalize the enterprise.
3. Expansion/diversification	Develop new projects; staff becomes semi-autonomous; the initial feel of small family business wanes; links with other institutions increase; organization becomes more complex.
4. Coordination	Redevelop communication systems for new diversity, formalize planning, define implementation strategies and methods and procedures for reporting.
5. Reformulation	Simplify systems, restore central purpose, balance the variety of purposes and services.

Just as pre-adolescence is not altogether distinct from adolescence, neither is stage two distinct from stage three or four from five. If you think about it, most often an organization is predominantly in one of the above stages. Since the stages tend to follow (not quite as night follows day), what you ought to be doing for the next stage can be predicted with some accuracy. But of course don't do that predicting without your colleague board members. Yet another strong initial discussion for your board.

WATCH OVER YOUR COMMUNITY

Yes, we said community not organization. You do have a community citizen hat as well as a board president one. And while all these pages have been directed at you wearing your presidential hat we would like to end more broadly. Both you and your organization, after all, do exist in a broader community of people and organizations. It is about that greater good that we now ask you to think. In doing so we acknowledge this is all far closer to philosophy than practicality, but then effective presidential leadership surely encompasses both. So stick with us here and you just may wish to try this conversation with your executive and your board.

The highest good probably is not pure organizational authenticity but something often identified as community or common good. An organization can be mission-faithful and ethically clean, and at the same time altogether absorbed in its own life. For human beings in infancy and severe personal trauma, self-absorption is necessary, even acceptable. Likewise, fresh new organizations and those in serious crisis understandably are self-absorbed and altogether internally focused. As an ongoing way of being, however, personal or organizational self-absorption is less than healthy and would not rate high in most systems of ethics.

So what does that philosophical excursion mean for your organization and you as president? At the least, it means that one of the challenges facing the leadership partners is near constant reference to the place and role of their organization in the overall scheme of things. It means doing what you do as an organization with integrity and excellence but also considering the impact of your action on the life of the broader community. It means a nearly constant balancing of organizational mission and priorities with the needs and priorities of the larger community of organizations. Perhaps most radically, it means a kind of organizational selflessness — versus self-absorption — that sometimes appears in the literature but seldom shows up in practice.

One organization refused to pursue a grant from a community foundation because in that moment of history a smaller colleague organization needed it more. Another organization decided not to initiate a new program direction because it would have constituted unfair (meaning more prestigious and powerful) competition with a smaller, more single-focused agency. Yet another urged a particularly effective board member to take a leave of absence and serve on the board of a colleague organization struggling through a painful personnel problem. Organizational selflessness just may grow to be as common and newsworthy as often-reported accounts of personal selflessness.

Not-for-profit organizations are special by law and also by purpose. And while there is much written about what they can learn from the private sector, there is little discussion about what they contribute. A whole body of argument deals with how many people are employed in not-for-profits and, therefore, how much is contributed to the general economy. There is also the quality-of-life argument wherein not-for-profits assist in creating an environment in which business can grow and prosper. Both have value but neither gets at the special gifts that not-for-profits can bring to the community of organizations.

Perhaps the special gift has to do with a different kind of bottom line. Traditional for-profit corporations speak forcefully about the effect of salaries, capital expense and marketing on the bottom line. That bottom line has to do with the financial balance sheet and the need to return earnings to shareholders. That is the final end product, the goal of all else.

What is that goal for not-for-profits? While there are not shareholders, there is a balance sheet important to keep out of the red. But that probably is not the most important bottom line. We propose a notion that may contribute to balance, perspective and sanity. From for-profits we have learned the importance of focus and market niche. Perhaps what we give back for the good of the community is peripheral vision. For market niche can degenerate to singleness of purpose and then to organizational isolation and self-absorption. Peripheral vision is not merely fixing your gaze on your own balance sheet, but paying attention to the fortunes of others. It is the attitude of the common good under which, and by which, you ultimately judge all your organizational efforts. It renounces organizational imperialism in favor of organizational connectedness. It pays close attention to the well-being of other community groups and institutions. The concept of peripheral vision goes beyond seeing broadly to acting broadly for others.

We cannot imagine what that might be like in your own organizational situation. We can imagine, with the press of your own institutional agendas, that the concept of organizational selflessness has yet to emerge in your collective consciousness. Our experience is that some not-for-profits operate quite continually with the self-image of sacrifice: the salaries are low, the clients are predominantly underprivileged, the measurable successes are few. However, many of those same conditions have an insulating and separating consequence which, while understandable, works against a wider vision and a healthier community.

And so, we end with more than the singularity of an individual organization. And as we challenged you to think of your presidency as a partnership not merely with your board and executive, we challenge you to think of your organization's life in broad partnerships beyond the well-being of your own particular mission. We ourselves hope for a connectedness in serving and a willingness to modify pure organizational interest for the good of the broader community. That value carried into the rich and diverse community of organizations that exist in any city may be the special gift that the not-for-profit world gives to all our citizens.

After Words

Six Distinctive Voices

W̶e wanted to end with a personal word to you as president (or is it president-elect?). As board presidents ourselves, we have outlined, edited, and even heartily debated over what most we wanted to say to you and how to say it. Like you, each of us has our own special, sometimes peculiar, way of handling the board presidency. Each of us has, as do you, a distinctive voice and it is with those voices we'd like to end — a way for each one of us to pass on to you our closing thoughts. So with advance thanks for listening, here are our after words.

"The greatest leaders I know are comfortable in their own skin. They accept their own fallibility and do not attempt to inhabit someone else's version of a leader. My advice: be authentic, be bold, and bring all of yourself to the party."
— Donna Alvarado

"In a nonprofit setting, you can't just make people do stuff by assigning tasks. You have to motivate people to work for the organization. That requires forming real friendships with the board members and getting them to 'own' the problems and goals."
— Alan Radnor

"Listening comes first. Understanding what the board members care about and want for the organization and making sure they get that expressed is of primary importance. Then you have to develop a genuine partnership and rapport with your executive director."
— Kathy Ransier

"Above all else, as board president you need the courage to take hold and fix the things that don't work. Being true to the mission of the organization and having faith in the future — that's what should guide your actions as president."
— Warren Tyler

"The biggest challenges are the ones that, when addressed, bring the greatest rewards. Believe in the mission and find an effective and inspirational way to articulate that belief. Develop the ability to bring the staff and board together to keep the vision fresh and alive. Throughout all, maintain a sense of fun."
— Teckie Shackleford

"Some of the richest rewards and greatest challenges for a board president flow from forging workable solutions out of strong diversity of opinion. Be careful not to turn away from ideas inconsistent with your own. Be willing to listen carefully, always looking for the bridges that will link all board members to what is best for the organization."
— Carole Williams